Mastering Basic Skills™
First Grade
Helping Children Succeed!
D0568490

2
3
+6
11
?
!
played
th

ISBN 1-60022-078-9

# Table of Contents

# Table of Contents

# Contents by Skill

# Contents by Skill

# Introduction

Welcome to *Mastering Basic Skills*. First grade is the year when many children seem to have boundless energy and an incredible desire to learn. Six- and seven-year-olds are thrilled with their emerging ability to read and their heightened mathematical sense. Suddenly, they feel a sense of independence as they practice and perform all their new skills. This book helps reinforce the essential skills learned in first grade through short, fun, and educationally sound activities.

Although six- and seven-year-olds are eager to learn, they also believe that the world revolves around them. It is one of the most egocentric times in a child's life. It is difficult for children at this age to be patient or to delay a response. They simply want every thing and anything immediately. They want to be the best and the first at everything and anything they attempt.

Unfortunately, the world does not always let us be the best or the first, and many six- and seven-year-olds experience high degrees of frustration. Some children will cry easily, while others will demonstrate various tension-releasing behaviors such as pouting, feet-stamping, willfulness, and inflexibility. When a parent recognizes why this behavior is happening and that this behavior is normal, the parent is much more likely to deal with it effectively. Distract and redirect your child into a positive experience. Guide him into a successful moment. Be patient and help teach your child how to be patient. Show him how to express frustration in positive ways and not through negative behaviors.

Although this year is filled with some challenges, it is also a time when children develop a positive self-concept. They learn how to show respect to others and how to respect themselves. Six- and seven-year-olds are becoming more verbally self-expressive and are better able to interpret the feelings of others. They make mistakes, but they are also able to understand and learn from their mistakes.

This is a year when children also become attached to their teachers and seek constant approval from their parents. They need and crave adult guidance, affection, and praise. Enjoy your first grader! Be proud of his accomplishments! Provide constant encouragement!

# Everyday Ways to Enrich Learning Experiences

## Language Arts

The single most important skill that a child needs for success in school, and later in life, is to be "literate." In other words, children must learn how to read. You can do many things to encourage literacy.

- Read to your child every day.
- Talk about the pictures.
- Ask questions.
- Ask your child to guess what is going to happen next.
- Encourage your child to retell favorite stories or favorite parts of a story.
- Have your child make up a new ending for a story.
- Go to the library and let your child choose new books.
- Listen to your child read.
- Write stories together. Have your child illustrate the stories.
- Play listening games. Ask your child to identify words that share the same sound: initial sounds, ending sounds, vowel sounds, and so on.
- Have your child identify words in the environment, such as on street signs and billboards, in the names of stores, and so on.
- Fill your child's environment with literacy materials like magnetic letters, books, magazines, newspapers, catalogs, paper, pencils, crayons, paints, and CDs of children's music or recorded children's stories.
- Encourage children to "draw" or "write" thank-you notes or letters.
- Together make a scrapbook of first grade memories.

## Math & Science

So many toys and puzzles provide young children with early math and science learning experiences. Remember to point out all the ways we use numbers and science in our daily lives. Here are some suggested materials and activities:

- Magnifying glass
- Blocks, puzzles, and other building materials
- Magnets and magnetic numerals
- Scales (concepts of "heavier" and "lighter")
- Calculators and toy cash registers
- Have your child practice using numbers "in his head" (mental math). For example: "If you had three cats and one more cat came to visit, how many cats did you have in all? What if two of those cats ran away?"
- Visit science and children's museums.
- Talk about how we use numbers in the real world: telling time, buying groceries, paying bills, and so on.
- Take walks and observe nature.

# Fun Web Sites for First Graders

http://members.learningplanet.com/directory/index.asp?lev=2
Site includes math games, crossword and word search puzzles, memory match games, and word games.

http://www.nhtsa.dot.gov/kids/
Site provides a fun format for learning about safety. Crash test dummies guide visitors through Safety City, where they can learn about bus safety, bike safety, EMS teams, and more.

http://www.cogcon.com/gamegoo/gooey.html
Intermediate level games cover letter-sound correspondences and sentence word order. Advanced level games cover spelling, antonyms, synonyms, and poetry concepts.

http://www.planetpals.com
Cute characters teach kids facts about the earth, recycling, pre-cycling, Earth Day, the weather, and more.

http://www.smokeybear.com
At this site, visitors can learn about forest fires, campfire safety, and the history of Smokey Bear. Site also includes a story maker, printable pictures to color, and fun games and mazes.

http://www.crayola.com/kids/index.cfm
Site features creative art project ideas, printable activity pages, and e-cards to send. Online games include color matching, jigsaw puzzles, and more.

http://www.scholastic.com/kids
Site features games, news, a card factory, and polls. Kids can find their favorite story characters here.

http://www.bookadventure.org/ki/index.asp
The "Book Finder" feature helps kids find books that are just right for them, based on reading level and specific topics entered by the child. Some site features require free registration.

http://www.nick.com/games/
Find fun games with Nickelodeon's favorite characters.

http://www.prongo.com/games/ages6-9.html
Site includes fun math games, puzzles, word finds, memory games, and mazes. Also includes brainteasers, jokes, e-cards, and more.

http://www.animaland.org
This site is sponsored by ASPCA. It includes fun games, animal trivia, e-cards, screen savers, and more. Visitors can learn about all kinds of animals, the importance of proper pet care, and submit their questions about animals.

http://www.nwf.org/kids/index.html
Kids who visit this site of the National Wildlife Federation are greeted by Ranger Rick, the raccoon. Site includes a variety of games, outdoor activity suggestions, and fun virtual tours of important biology and ecology concepts.

http://oaklandzoo.org/
Kids can tour the animals at the Oakland Zoo from A to Z. Site also includes pictures and facts about the animals, as well as some sound and video clips.

http://www.moma.org/destination/
This site of the Museum of Modern Art in New York will take your child on a tour of the art museum. Questions guide children to look at several works of art. Children can also play games and do activities related to the works of art.

# Recommended Books for First Graders

**A**

*The Adventures of Laura and Jack* by Laura Ingalls Wilder
*The Ant and the Elephant* by Bill Peet
*Are You My Mother?* by P.D. Eastman
*Arthur's Camp-Out* by Lillian Hoban
*Arthur's Family Vacation* by Marc Brown
*Arthur's First Sleepover* by Marc Brown
*Arthur's Neighborhood* by Marc Brown
*Arthur's Teacher Trouble* by Marc Brown
*Aunt Eater's Mystery Vacation* by Doug Cushman

**B**

*Baseball Brothers* by Jean, Dan, and Dave Marzollo
*A Bear for Miguel* by Elaine Marie Alphin
*Bear's Hiccups* by Marion Dane Bauer
*Best Friends* by Marcia Leonard
*Best Friends for Frances* by Russell Hoban
*The Best Way to Play* by Bill Cosby
*Big Bad Bruce* by Bill Peet
*The Boy with the Helium Head* by Phyllis Reynolds Naylor
*Bright Lights, Little Gerbil* by Stephanie Spinner and Ellen Weiss
*Buffalo Bill and the Pony Express* by Eleanor Coerr
*Buford, the Little Bighorn* by Bill Peet

**C**

*The Caboose Who Got Loose* by Bill Peet
*Cam Jansen and the Triceratops Pops Mystery* by David A. Adler
*Cinderella*, illustrated by Marcia Brown
*Come Down Now, Flying Cow!* by Timothy Roland
*Commander Toad and the Voyage Home* by Jane Yolen

**D**

*Danny and the Dinosaur Go to Camp* by Syd Hoff
*Do You Want to Be My Friend?* by Eric Carle
*The Dog That Called the Pitch* by Matt Christopher
*Don't Forget the Bacon!* by Pat Hutchins

**F**

*Father Bear Comes Home* by Else Holmelund Minarik, illustrated by Maurice Sendak
*Five Little Monkeys Jumping on the Bed*, retold and illustrated by Eileen Christelow
*Flossie and the Fox* by Patricia C. McKissack
*Frog and Toad All Year* by Arnold Lobel
*Frog and Toad Are Friends* by Arnold Lobel
*Funnybones* by Janet and Allan Ahlberg

**G**

*The Gingerbread Boy* by Paul Galdone
*The Golly Sisters Ride Again* by Betsy Byars
*Good Night, Good Knight* by Shelley Moore Thomas
*Good-night, Owl!* by Pat Hutchins
*Gorky Rises* by William Steig

**H**

*Harold and the Purple Crayon* by Crockett Johnson
*Henry and Mudge and Annie's Perfect Pet: The Twentieth Book of Their Adventures* by Cynthia Rylant
*Henry and Mudge and the Sneaky Crackers: The Sixteenth Book of Their Adventures* by Cynthia Rylant
*Higglety Pigglety Pop! Or, There Must Be More to Life* by Maurice Sendak
Hour of the Olympics by Mary Pope Osborne

**I**

*I Know an Old Lady Who Swallowed a Fly*, retold and illustrated by Nadine Bernard Westcott
*If You Give a Moose a Muffin* by Laura Joffe Numeroff
*If You Give a Mouse a Cookie* by Laura Joffe Numeroff
*Inside, Outside, Upside Down* by Stan and Jan Berenstain
*Ira Sleeps Over* by Bernard Waber

**J**

*Jethro and Joel Were a Troll* by Bill Peet
*Joshua James Likes Trucks* by Catherine Petrie

**L**

*Last One in Is a Rotten Egg* by Leonard Kessler
*Lightning Liz* by Larry Dane Brimner
*Lilly's Purple Plastic Purse* by Kevin Henkes
*Little Wolf, Big Wolf* by Matt Novak

**M**

*Make Way for Ducklings* by Robert McCloskey
*Mama's Birthday Surprise* by Elizabeth Spurr
*Marmee's Surprise: A Little Women Story*, adapted by Monica Kulling, based on the novel by Louisa May Alcott
*Meow!*, retold and illustrated by Katya Arnold
*Messy Bessey* by Patricia and Frederick McKissack
*Mike Mulligan and His Steam Shovel* by Virginia Lee Burton
*Miss Nelson Is Missing!* by Harry Allard and James Marshall
*The Mitten: A Ukrainian Folktale*, adapted and illustrated by Jan Brett
*The Mixed-up Chameleon* by Eric Carle
*Monkey Trouble* by David Martin
*Mouse Mess* by Linnea Riley
*My Brother, Ant* by Betsy Byars
*My Name Is María Isabel* by Alma Flor Ada

**N**

*Nate the Great and Me: The Case of the Fleeing Fang* by Marjorie Weinman Sharmat
*No Jumping on the Bed!* by Tedd Arnold

**O**

*Ox-Cart Man* by Donald Hall

**P**

*Petunia* by Roger Duvoisin
*Picnic with Piggins* by Jane Yolen
*Pinky and Rex and the New Baby* by James Howe
*Pioneer Cat* by William H. Hooks
*Play Ball, Amelia Bedelia* by Peggy Parish
*The Polar Express* by Chris Van Allsburg

**R**

*The Rainbow Fish* by Marcus Pfister
*Rats on the Roof and Other Stories* by James Marshall
*The Relatives Came* by Cynthia Rylant
*Roland, the Minstrel Pig* by William Steig
*Rooster's Off to See the World* by Eric Carle
*Rosie's Walk* by Pat Hutchins

**S**

*Silver Packages: An Appalachian Christmas Story* by Cynthia Rylant
*Skip to My Lou*, adapted and illustrated by Nadine Bernard Westcott
*Sleep-Over Mouse* by Mary Packard
*Smasher* by Dick King-Smith
*Something Queer in the Cafeteria* by Elizabeth Levy
*Song and Dance Man* by Karen Ackerman
*Song Lee and the Hamster Hunt* by Suzy Kline
*Stone Soup: An Old Tale*, retold and illustrated by Marcia Brown
*The Stories Huey Tells* by Ann Cameron
*The Story of Ferdinand* by Munro Leaf
*Strega Nona: An Old Tale*, retold and illustrated by Tomie de Paola
*Strega Nona's Magic Lessons* by Tomie de Paola

**T**

*The Tales of Peter Rabbit and Benjamin Bunny*, adapted by Sindy McKay from the stories of Beatrix Potter
*Three by the Sea* by Edward Marshall
*Time for Bed?* by Susan Hood
*The Three Little Pigs*, illustrated by Eileen Grace
*The Town Mouse and the Country Mouse*, retold and illustrated by Helen Craig

**V**

*Veronica* by Roger Duvoisin
*The Very Busy Spider* by Eric Carle
*The Very Clumsy Click Beetle* by Eric Carle
*The Very Hungry Caterpillar* by Eric Carle
*The Very Quiet Cricket* by Eric Carle

**W**

*Wizard and Wart in Trouble* by Janice Lee Smith
*Wolfmen Don't Hula Dance* by Debbie Dadey and Marcia Thornton Jones

# First Grade Skills Checklist

This list is an overview of some of the key skills learned in first grade. When using this list, please keep in mind that the curriculum will vary across the United States, as will how much an individual teacher is able to teach over the course of one year. The list will give you an overview of the majority of first grade skills and assist you in motivating, guiding, and helping your child maintain or even increase skills over vacation.

## Language Arts/Reading

- Recognizes uppercase letters ❑
- Recognizes lowercase letters ❑
- Can print uppercase letters correctly ❑
- Can print lowercase letters correctly ❑
- Knows alphabetical sequence ❑
- Recognizes beginning consonant sounds ❑
- Recognizes final consonant sounds ❑
- Recognizes short vowel sounds ❑
- Recognizes long vowel sounds ❑
- Knows L blends: bl, cl, fl, gl, pl, sl ❑
- Knows beginning blends: sk, sm, sn, sp, st, sw, tw ❑
- Knows R blends: br, cr, dr, fr, gr, pr, tr ❑
- Knows digraphs: ch, sh, th, ng ❑
- Recognizes r-controlled vowels: ar, er, ir, or, ur ❑
- Can sound out simple words ❑
- Can identify characters in a story ❑
- Can identify the main idea of a story ❑
- Can identify the setting of a story ❑
- Can identify the conclusion of a story ❑
- Uses letter sounds to write words ❑
- Draws illustrations to match sentences ❑
- Can identify compound words ❑
- Can identify nouns ❑
- Can identify proper nouns ❑
- Can identify pronouns ❑
- Can identify verbs ❑
- Can identify linking verbs: am, is, are, was, were ❑
- Uses punctuation correctly: period, question mark, exclamation point ❑
- Recognizes rhyming words ❑
- Recognizes antonyms, synonyms, and homonyms ❑
- Is beginning to read and write for pleasure ❑

## Math

- Counts and recognizes numbers to 100 ❑
- Counts by 2s to 100 ❑
- Counts by 5s to 100 ❑
- Counts by 10s to 100 ❑
- Completes simple patterns ❑
- Sorts by one or two attributes ❑
- Can sequence events ❑
- Can name eight basic shapes ❑
- Knows addition facts to 10 ❑
- Knows subtraction facts to 10 ❑
- Can write number sentences using +, –, and = ❑
- Knows addition facts to 18 ❑
- Knows subtraction facts to 18 ❑
- Can read and create a graph ❑
- Knows ordinal numbers (first–tenth) ❑
- Reads number words ❑
- Understands place value in the ones place ❑
- Understands place value in the tens place ❑
- Understands place value in the hundreds place ❑
- Adds two-digit numbers, no regrouping ❑
- Subtracts two-digit numbers, no regrouping ❑
- Adds three-digit numbers, no regrouping ❑
- Subtracts three-digit numbers, no regrouping ❑
- Performs column addition with three single-digit numbers ❑
- Recognizes money: penny, nickel, dime, quarter, half-dollar ❑
- Knows the value of money: penny, nickel, dime, quarter, half-dollar ❑
- Can count money using pennies, nickels, and dimes ❑
- Can perform money addition problems using a decimal point ❑
- Can tell time on the hour ❑
- Can tell time on the half hour ❑
- Can measure using inches ❑
- Can measure using centimeters ❑
- Can identify fractions: $1/2$, $1/3$, $1/4$ ❑
- Uses problem-solving strategies to complete math problems ❑

# First Grade Word Lists

after
all
am
and
animal
are
at

be
because
best
big
boy
brother
but

can
can't
car
children
come

day
did
do
down

eat

favorite
for
friend
from
fun

get
girl
give
go
good

had
has
have
he
her
here
him
his
house
how

I
in
is
it

jump

kick

like
little
look

made
make
me
my

new
nice
night
no
not

of
off
old
on
out
over

people
play
pretty

quit

rain
ride

said
saw
school
see
she
sister
some

talk
teacher
tell
that
the
them
there
they
thing
this
to

up
us

very

want
was
we
went
what
when
where
who
why
will
with
won't

you
your

zoo

## Long Vowels

### Initial a

able
acre
agent
apex
April
apron
Asia

### Initial e

ecology
equal
ether
even
evil

### Initial i

I
icy
idea
iodine
iris
item
ivory

### Initial o

obey
oboe
ocean
odor
okra
omit
open
over

### Initial u

uniform
unify
unique
unit
united
universe
university
usual
utilize

### Medial a

baby
basis
crazy
flavor
hazy
label
labor
ladle
lady
navy
paper
station
vapor

### Medial e

being
cedar
depot
female
legal
meter
prefix
recent
secret
zebra

### Medial i

bicycle
climate
dinosaur
giant
lion
pilot
rifle
silent
spider
tiny
title
triangle

### Medial o

broken
moment
October
poem
program
total

### Medial u

bugle
cubic
cupid
fuel
future
human
humid
humor
museum
puny
pupil

### Final e

be
he
maybe
me
she
we

### Final o

ago
also
cargo
echo
hello
hero
piano
volcano
zero

### Final u

emu
guru
menu
tutu

# Short Vowels

**Initial a**

act
add
after
alligator
alphabet
animal
answer
ant
antelope
apple
ask
astronaut
at
ax

**Initial e**

edge
egg
elbow
elephant
elevator
elf
elk
elm
envelope
Eskimo
ever
every
everyone
except
explain

**Initial i**

if
igloo
ill
in
inch
Indian
ink
insect
instrument
interest
introduce
invent
invite
it
itch

**Initial o**

October
octopus
odd
off
offer
office
olive
omelet
operation
ostrich
otter
ox
oxygen

**Initial u**

ugly
umbrella
uncle
uncover
under
underwear
undress
unhappy
until
up
us

**Medial a**

bag
band
basket
bat
batch
cab
can
cat
class
crab
dad
fan
fat
flag
gas
glass
grab
grass
had
ham
hand
hat
hatch
patch
path
quack
ranch
scratch
spank
stack
tracks

**Medial e**

bed
beg
bell
belt
bench
bent
best
bet
desk
guess
help
hen
jelly
jet
leg
let
men
nest
peg
pen
red
rest
set
sled
spell
spent
tent
vest
west
wet
when
yet

**Medial i**

bring
chin
dig
dish
ditch
fig
fish
fist
fit
grin
hid
hitch
kit
jig
lid
lift
limb
limp
lips
milk
mitt
mix
pick
pig
pin
pinch
ring
rip
ship
sick
silly
sing
sink
sip
six
skinny
sticks

**Medial o**

block
bog
box
chop
clock
clot
cloth
cob
cost
cot
dock
dog
doll
drop
flop
fog
fox
frog
golf
hog
hot
job
jog
lock
log
lost
lot
mop
moth
not
ox
pop
rob
rock
rocker
shop
sock
spot
stop
top
tot

**Medial u**

buck
bud
bug
bump
bunch
bus
cub
cuff
cup
cut
drum
duck
dump
dust
hug
hunt
jug
jump
just
luck
mud
mug
must
nuts
plum
rub
rug
run
rust
shrunk
skunk
stump
sunk
truck
trunk
tub

# Patterns

Continue each pattern.

## Symbols

1.  ______ ______ ______ ______

2.  ______ ______ ______ ______

3. ______ ______ ______ ______

4. ______ ______ ______ ______

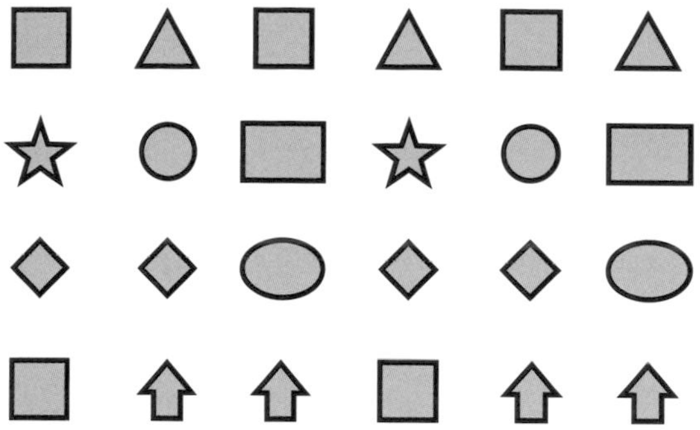

## Numbers

A. 1 2 1 2 1 2 ______ ______ ______ ______ ______ ______

B. 5 4 6 5 4 6 5 4 ______ ______ ______ ______ ______

C. 9 9 8 9 9 8 9 9 8 ______ ______ ______ ______ ______

D. 1 5 2 5 1 5 2 5 1 5 2 5 ______ ______ ______ ______

Now create your own patterns.

# Uppercase Letters

Trace and print the uppercase letters.

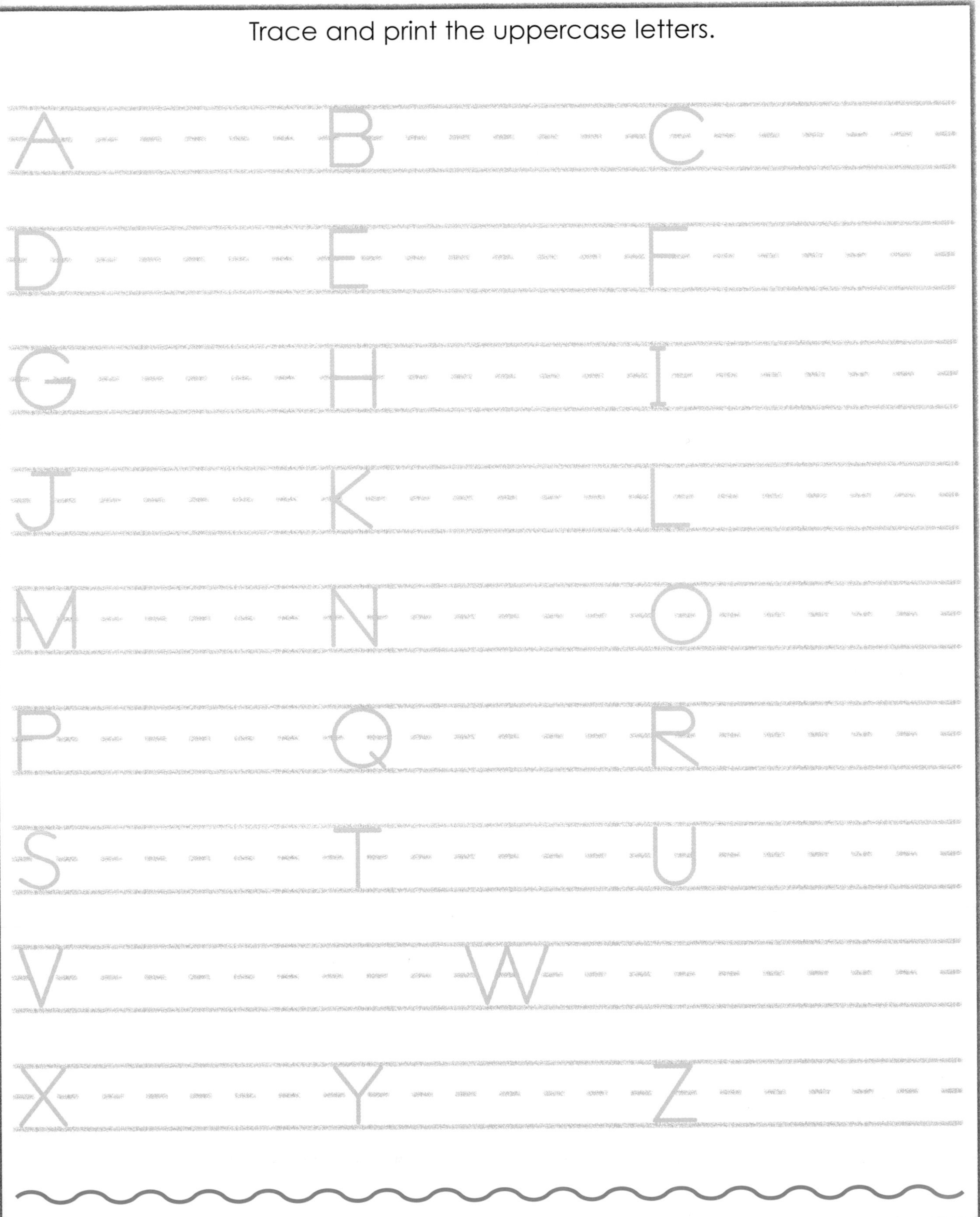

# Lowercase Letters

Trace and print the lowercase letters.

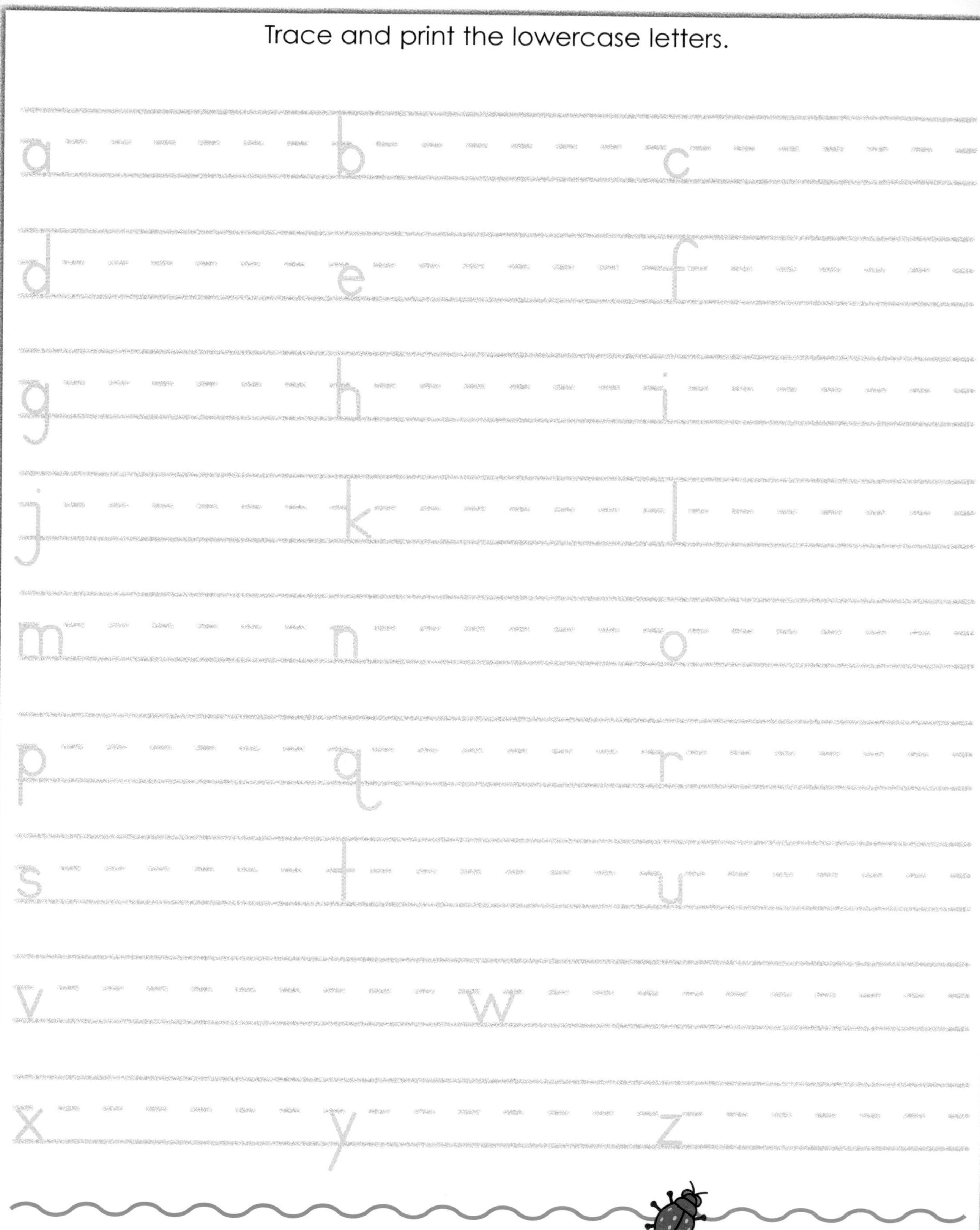

# Hundred Chart and Activities

| 1 | 2 | 3 | 4 | 5 | 6 | 7 | 8 | 9 | 10 |
|---|---|---|---|---|---|---|---|---|---|
| 11 | 12 | 13 | 14 | 15 | 16 | 17 | 18 | 19 | 20 |
| 21 | 22 | 23 | 24 | 25 | 26 | 27 | 28 | 29 | 30 |
| 31 | 32 | 33 | 34 | 35 | 36 | 37 | 38 | 39 | 40 |
| 41 | 42 | 43 | 44 | 45 | 46 | 47 | 48 | 49 | 50 |
| 51 | 52 | 53 | 54 | 55 | 56 | 57 | 58 | 59 | 60 |
| 61 | 62 | 63 | 64 | 65 | 66 | 67 | 68 | 69 | 70 |
| 71 | 72 | 73 | 74 | 75 | 76 | 77 | 78 | 79 | 80 |
| 81 | 82 | 83 | 84 | 85 | 86 | 87 | 88 | 89 | 90 |
| 91 | 92 | 93 | 94 | 95 | 96 | 97 | 98 | 99 | 100 |

**A.** Touch each number and say the number out loud.

**B.** String together 100 pieces of cereal, counting as you go.

**C.** Make a paper chain using 100 links.

# Beginning Consonant Review (Part 1)

Circle the correct beginning sound.

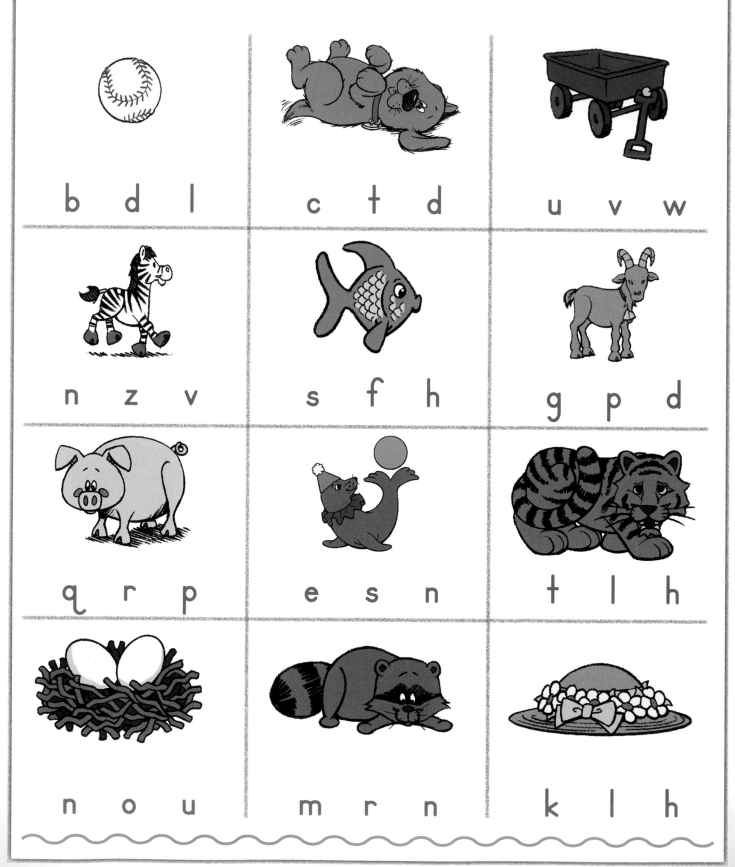

| | | |
|---|---|---|
|  b d l |  c t d |  u v w |
|  n z v |  s f h |  g p d |
|  q r p |  e s n |  t l h |
|  n o u |  m r n |  k l h |

# Counting by 1s

Help Fuzzy find her bone.
Start at 1. Count by 1s and trace your path.

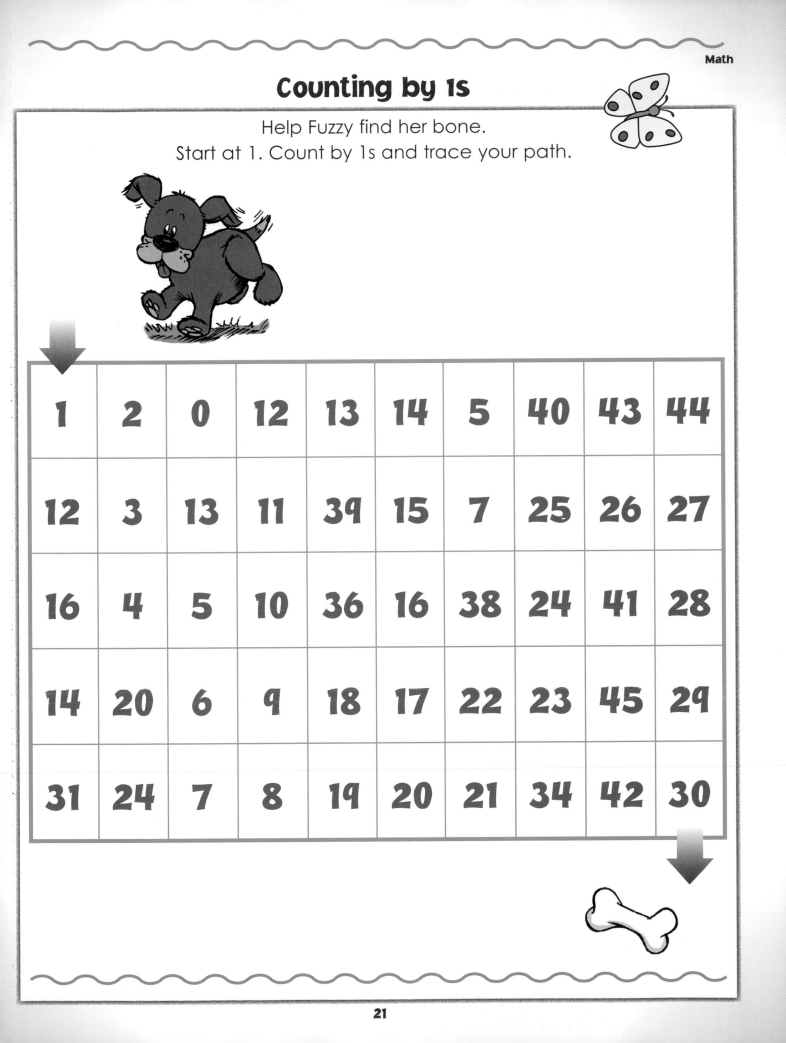

| 1 | 2 | 0 | 12 | 13 | 14 | 5 | 40 | 43 | 44 |
|---|---|---|---|---|---|---|---|---|---|
| 12 | 3 | 13 | 11 | 39 | 15 | 7 | 25 | 26 | 27 |
| 16 | 4 | 5 | 10 | 36 | 16 | 38 | 24 | 41 | 28 |
| 14 | 20 | 6 | 9 | 18 | 17 | 22 | 23 | 45 | 29 |
| 31 | 24 | 7 | 8 | 19 | 20 | 21 | 34 | 42 | 30 |

# Beginning Consonant Review (Part 2)

Circle the correct beginning sound.

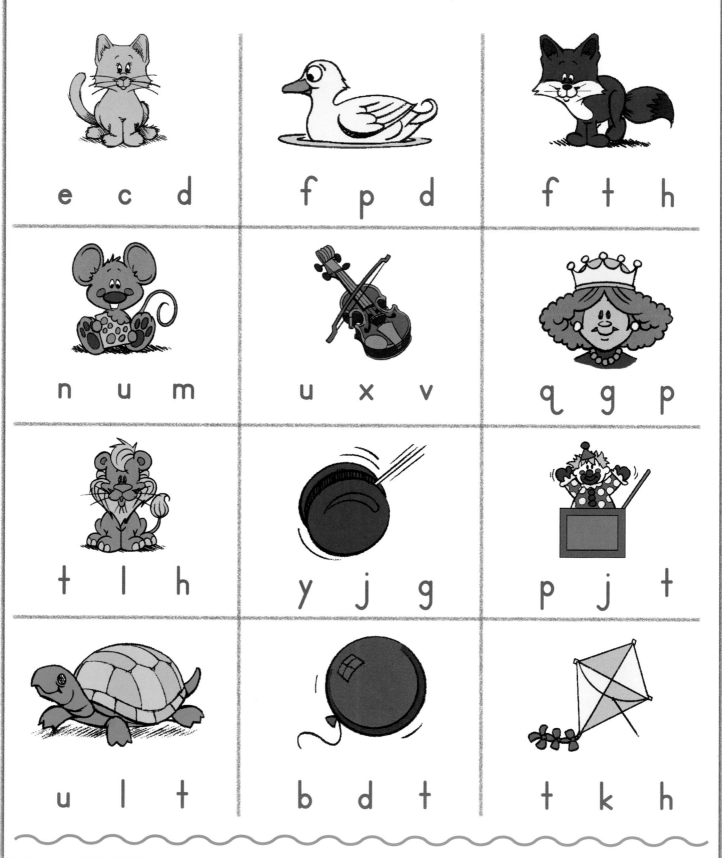

| | | |
|---|---|---|
| e c d | f p d | f t h |
| n u m | u x v | q g p |
| t l h | y j g | p j t |
| u l t | b d t | t k h |

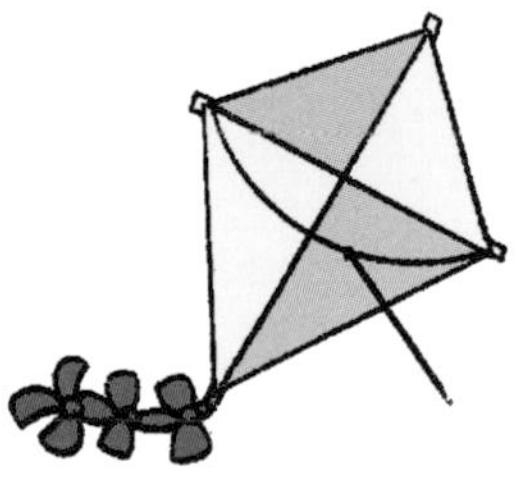

# Counting by 2s and 5s

Count by 2s. Fill in the missing numerals.

A.  2 ____ 6 ____ ____ 12

B.  14 ____ ____ 20 ____ ____

C.  ____ 30 ____ ____ 36 ____

D.  40 ____ ____ 46 ____ ____

Count by 5s. Fill in the missing numerals.

E.  5 ____ ____ 20 ____ ____

F.  35 ____ 45 ____ ____ ____

G.  70 ____ ____ 85 ____ ____

H.  55 ____ ____ ____ 75 ____

# Beginning Consonant Review (Part 3)

Write the correct beginning sound.

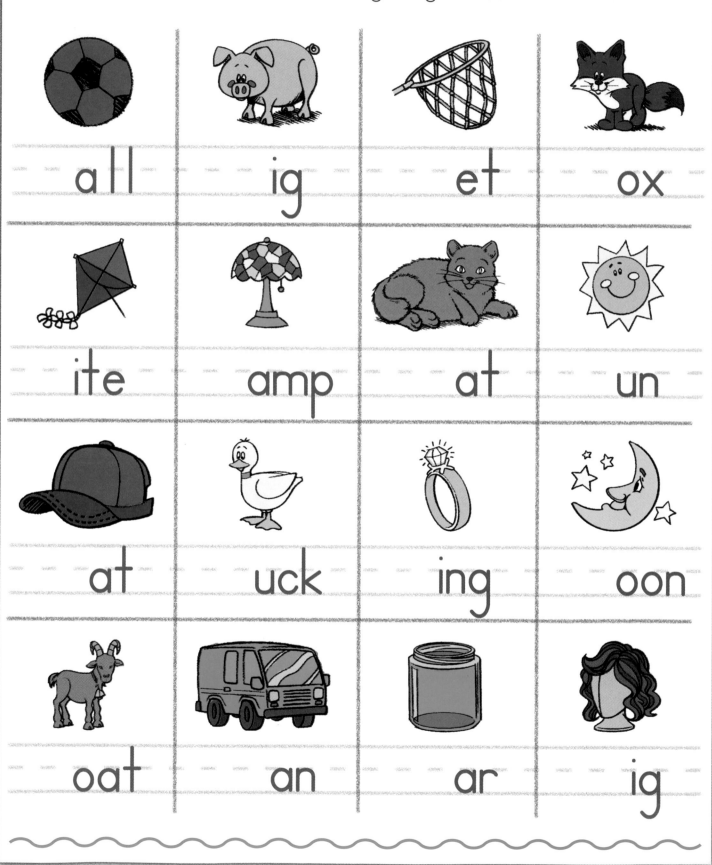

| | | | |
|---|---|---|---|
|  all |  ig | 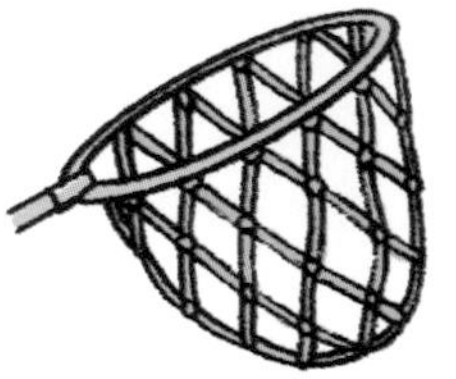 et |  ox |
|  ite |  amp |  at |  un |
|  at |  uck |  ing |  oon |
|  oat |  an |  ar |  ig |

# Ending Consonant Review

Circle the correct ending sound.

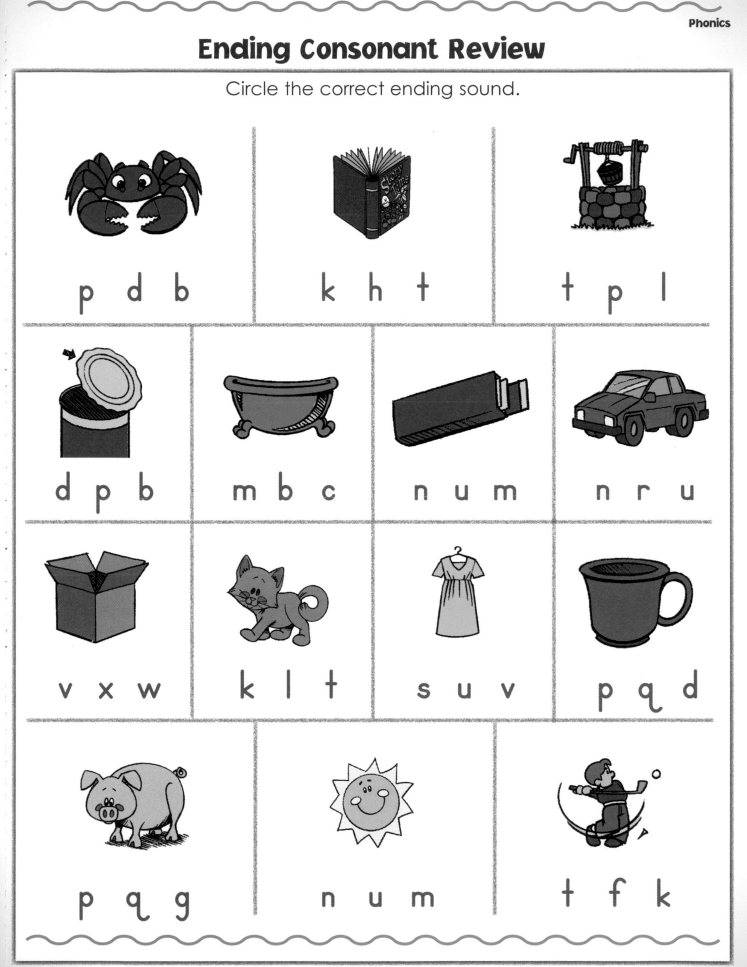

p d b

k h t

t p l

d p b

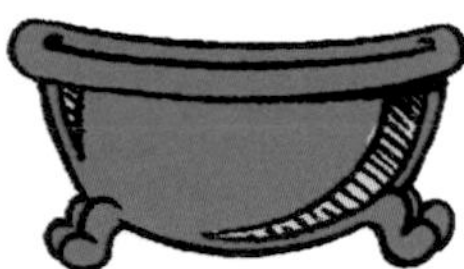

m b c

n u m

n r u

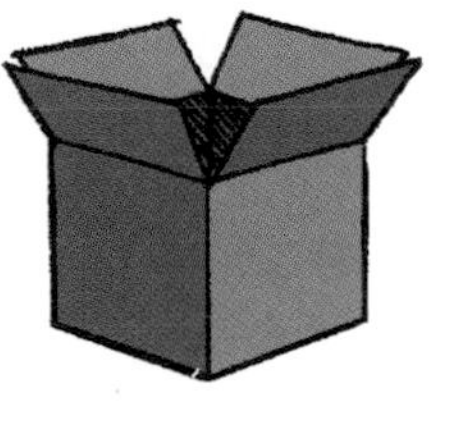

v x w

k l t

s u v

p q d

p q g

n u m

t f k

# Counting by 10s

Count by 10s. Fill in the missing numerals.

A.

10 _____ _____ 40 _____ 60 _____

B.

30 _____ _____ 60 _____ _____ _____

C.

_____ 50 _____ _____ _____ _____ 100

D.

20 _____ _____ 50 _____ _____ _____

E.

10 _____ 30 _____ _____ 60 _____

F.

_____ 50 _____ _____ 80 _____ 100

G.

_____ 40 _____ 60 _____ _____ 90

# Beginning and Ending Consonant Review

Write the correct beginning and ending sounds.

| | | | |
|---|---|---|---|
|  a |  i |  a |  o |
|  e |  u |  a | 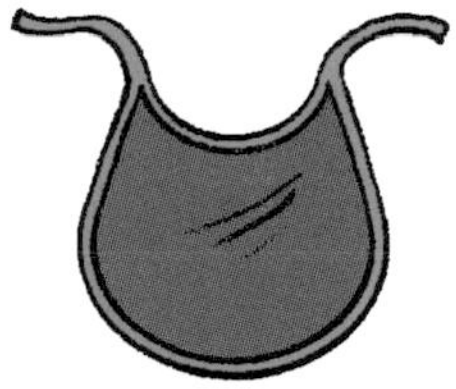 i |
|  i |  o |  e |  u |
|  e |  i |  o |  u |

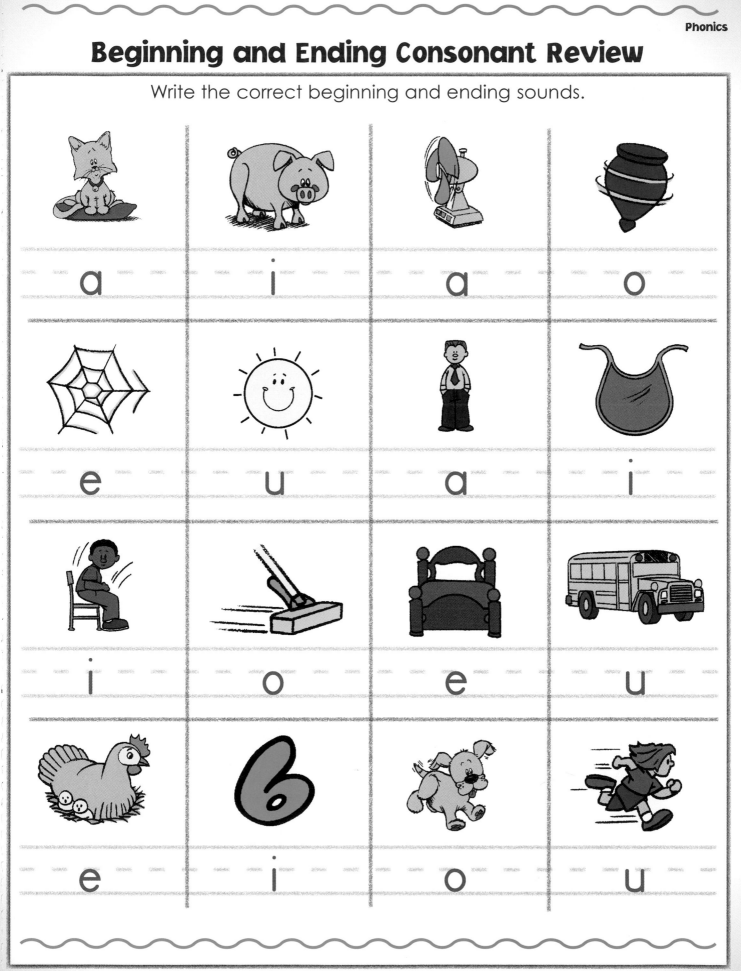

# Read and Color

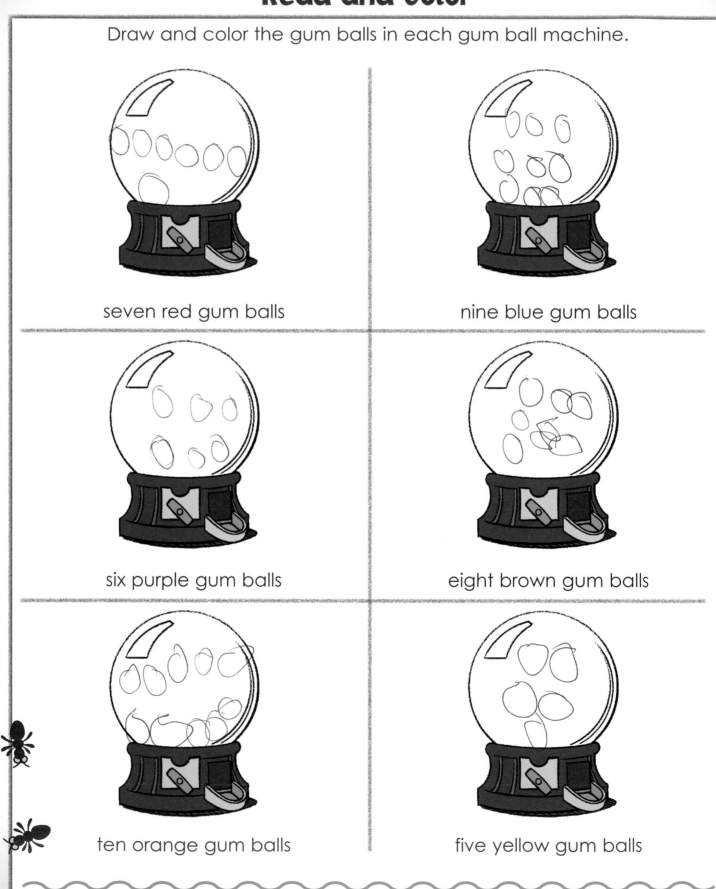

Draw and color the gum balls in each gum ball machine.

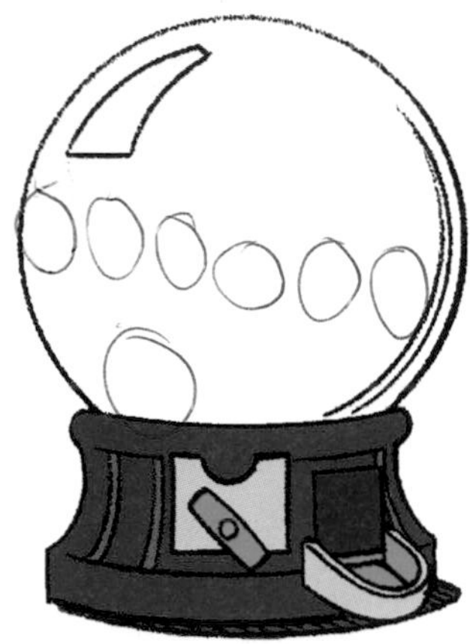

seven red gum balls

nine blue gum balls

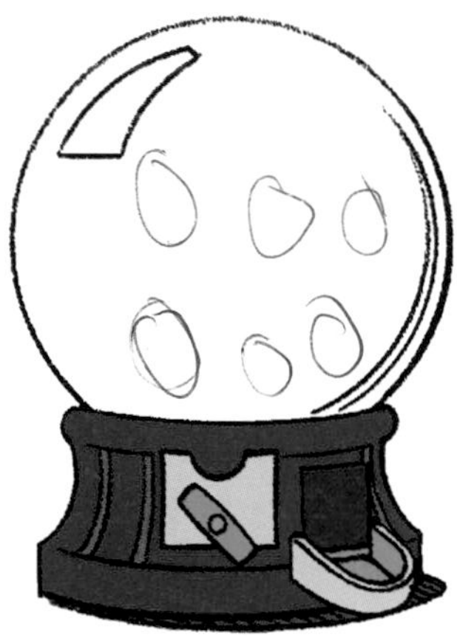

six purple gum balls

eight brown gum balls

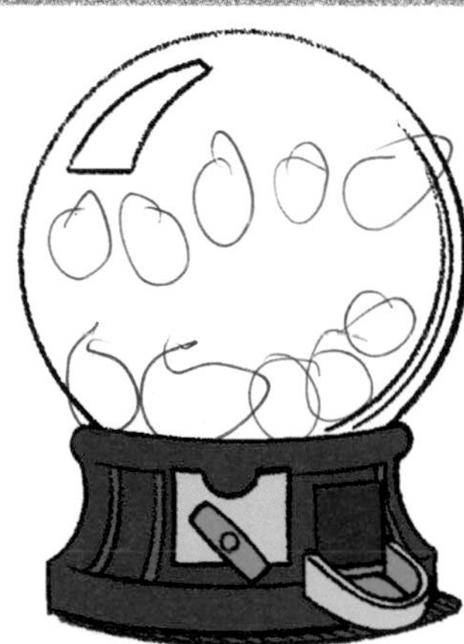

ten orange gum balls

five yellow gum balls

# Cut-and-Paste Respect

Cut out the eight squares at the bottom of the page. Paste each activity to show whether it demonstrates respect to self, property, others, or the environment.

| Self | Property | Others | Environment |
| --- | --- | --- | --- |
| | | | |
| | | | |

| | | | |
| --- | --- | --- | --- |
|  Return library books on time. |  Exercise. |  Put things back where they belong. |  Pick up litter. |
|  Share toys. |  Recycle. |  Eat healthy food. |  Take turns. |

Use the secret code to solve the riddle.

**Which side of a chicken has the most feathers?**

**The** ____ ____ ____ ____ ____ ____ ____

  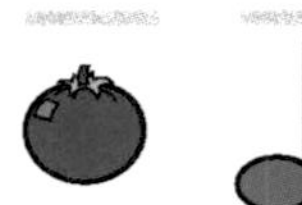  

## Secret Code

 = T   = O   = U

 = D  = S  = I

 = E



Remove pages 31–34. Cut along dashed lines. Staple pages in order.

# My Secret Code Riddle Book

By

Detective ____________________

Use the secret code to solve the riddle.

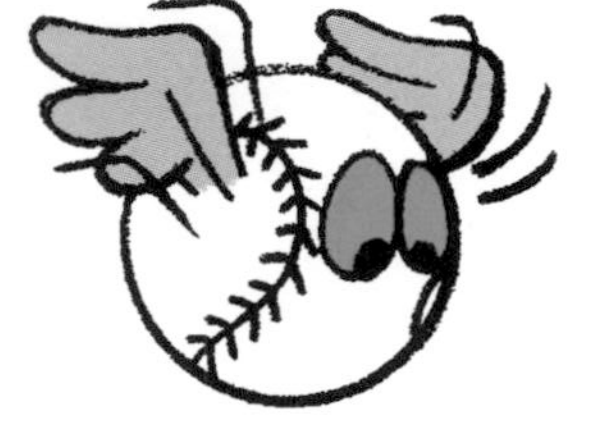

**What kind of animal is always found at a baseball game?**

**A** ___ ___ ___

## Secret Code

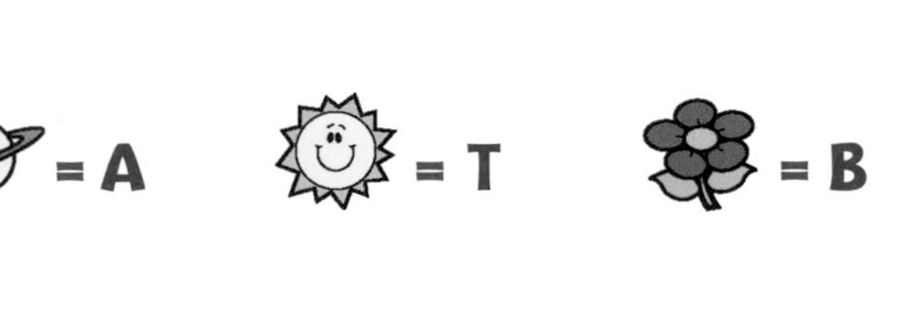




Use the secret code to solve the riddle.

**What kind of cup is good to eat?**

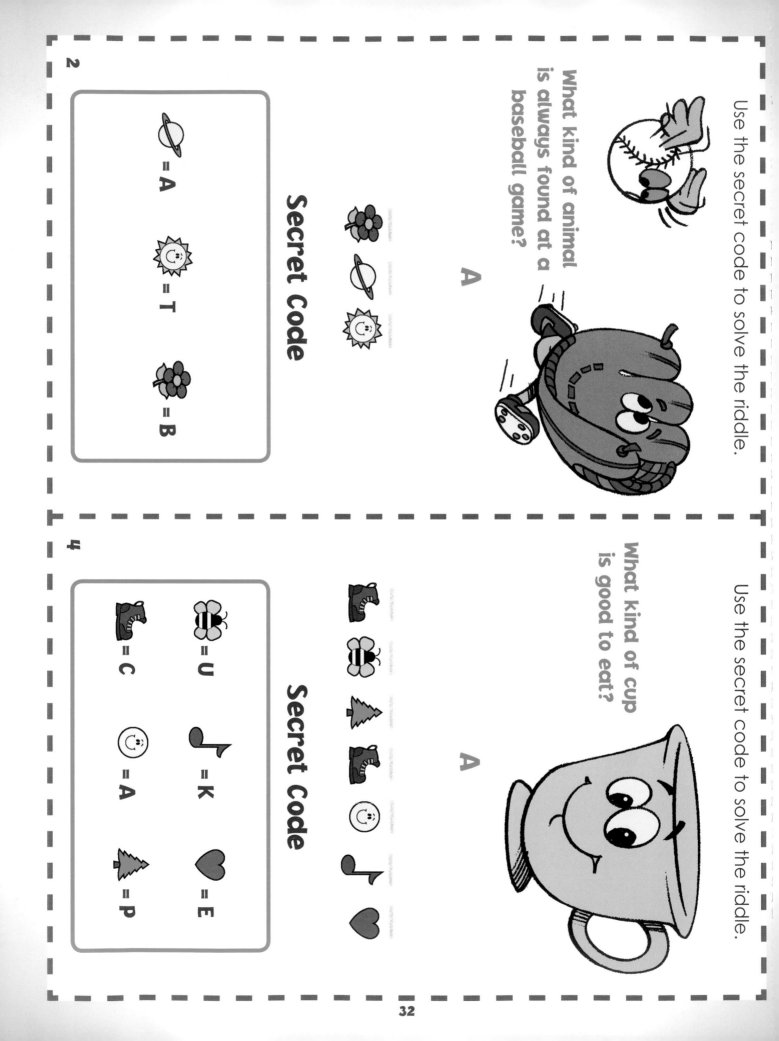

**A** ___ ___ ___ ___ ___ ___ ___

## Secret Code

 = C

= A

 = P

Use the secret code to solve the riddle.

**What do you call a sleeping bull?**

**A** ____ ____ ____ ____ ____ ____ ____ ____ ____

## Secret Code

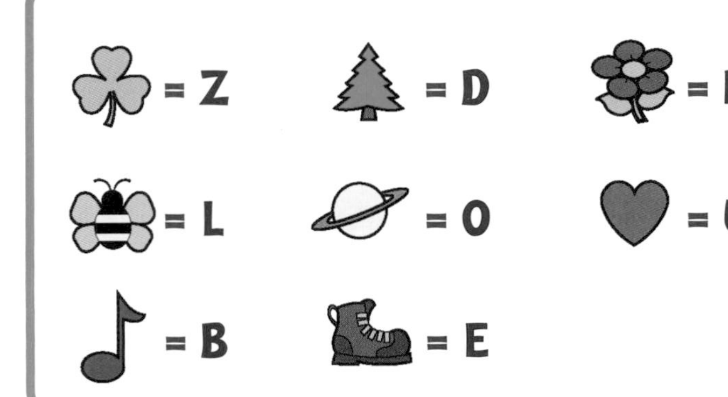


7

Use the secret code to solve the riddle.

**What did the cat say when the vet gave her a shot?**

____ ____ – ____ ____ !

## Secret Code

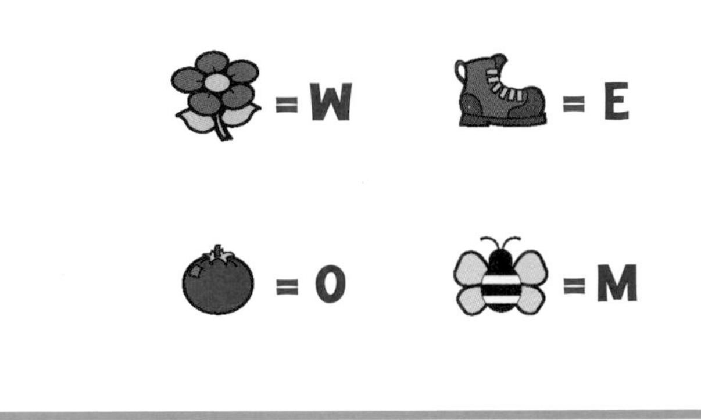


5

Use the secret code to solve the riddle.

**What kind of fish is rich?**

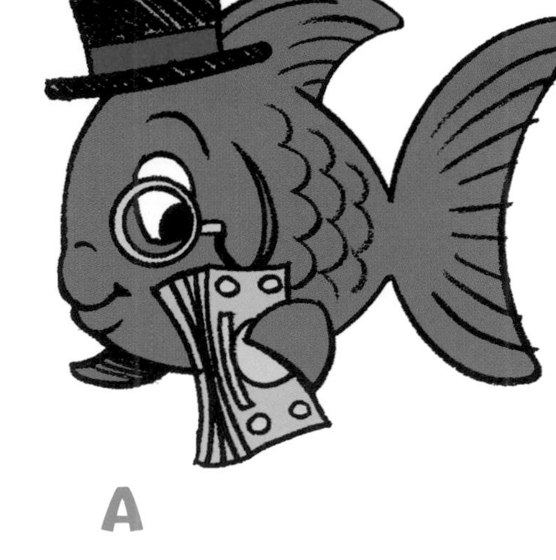

A

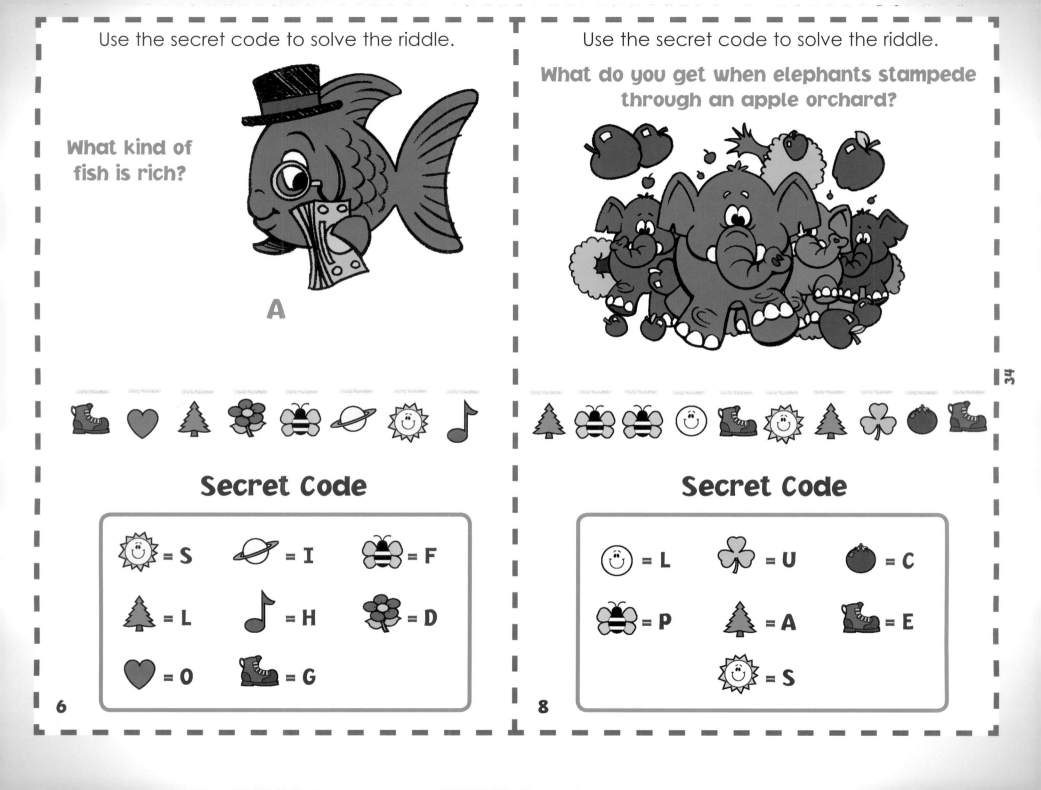

## Secret Code

6

Use the secret code to solve the riddle.

**What do you get when elephants stampede through an apple orchard?**

## Secret Code

8

# Nouns (Naming Words)

A **noun** is a word that names a person, place, or thing.

Cut and paste the picture of each noun where it belongs.

| Person | | Place | | Thing | |
|---|---|---|---|---|---|
| | | | | | |
| | | | | | |

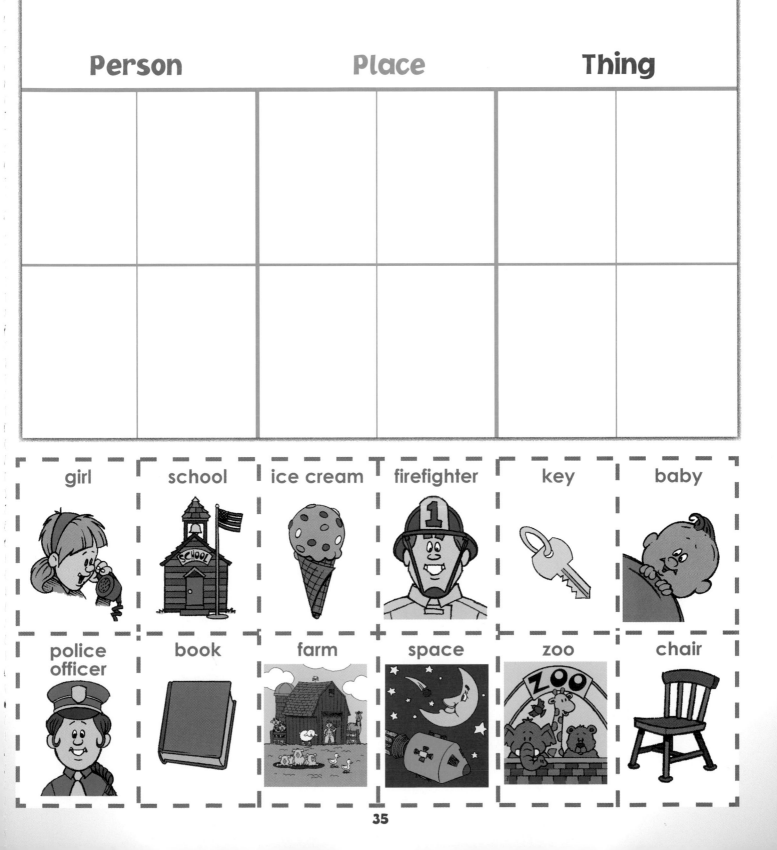

girl

school

ice cream

firefighter

key

baby

police officer

book

farm

space

zoo

chair

# Practice Using Nouns

Read each sentence. Write the correct noun from the word list on the line. You will not use all of the words.

**Word List**

| | | |
|---|---|---|
| baby | doctor | teacher |
| nest | school | chair |
| hospital | dentist | car |
| woods | pencil | cowboy |
| piano | apple | store |

1. This is a **thing** used to make music.
2. This **person** checks your teeth.
3. This **place** sells things you need.
4. This is a **thing** you use to write.
5. This **person** helps you learn at school.
6. This **place** is where children go to learn.
7. This is a **thing** in which a bird lays eggs.
8. This **person** works in a hospital.

# Story Web

Read your favorite story. Describe it by filling in the story web below with words, sentences, or pictures.

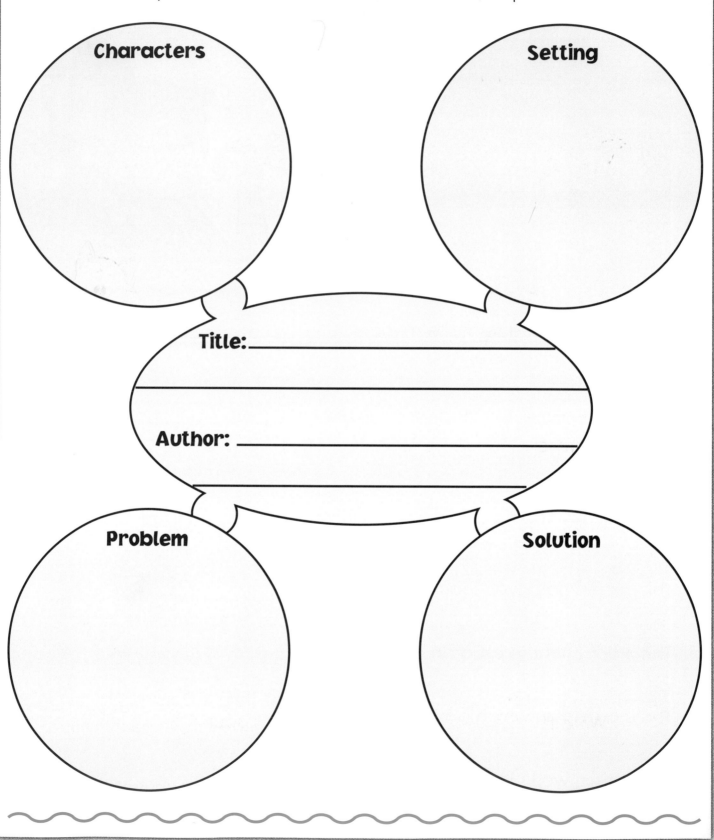

Characters

Setting

Title: ______________________________

______________________________

Author: ______________________________

______________________________

Problem

Solution

# Short ă

Say the words. Listen to the short sound of the vowel **a**.

**căp**  **băg** 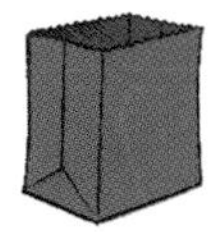 **căn** 

Color the pictures that have the **ă** vowel sound.

Draw the ˘ symbol above the **a**. Match each word to the correct picture.

**fan**

**hat**

**lamp**

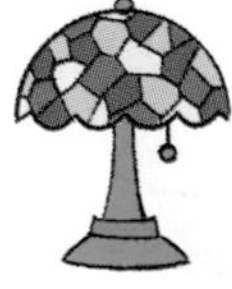

Write three words that have the short **ă** sound as in **pan**.

# Color by Code

Add. Color using the code.

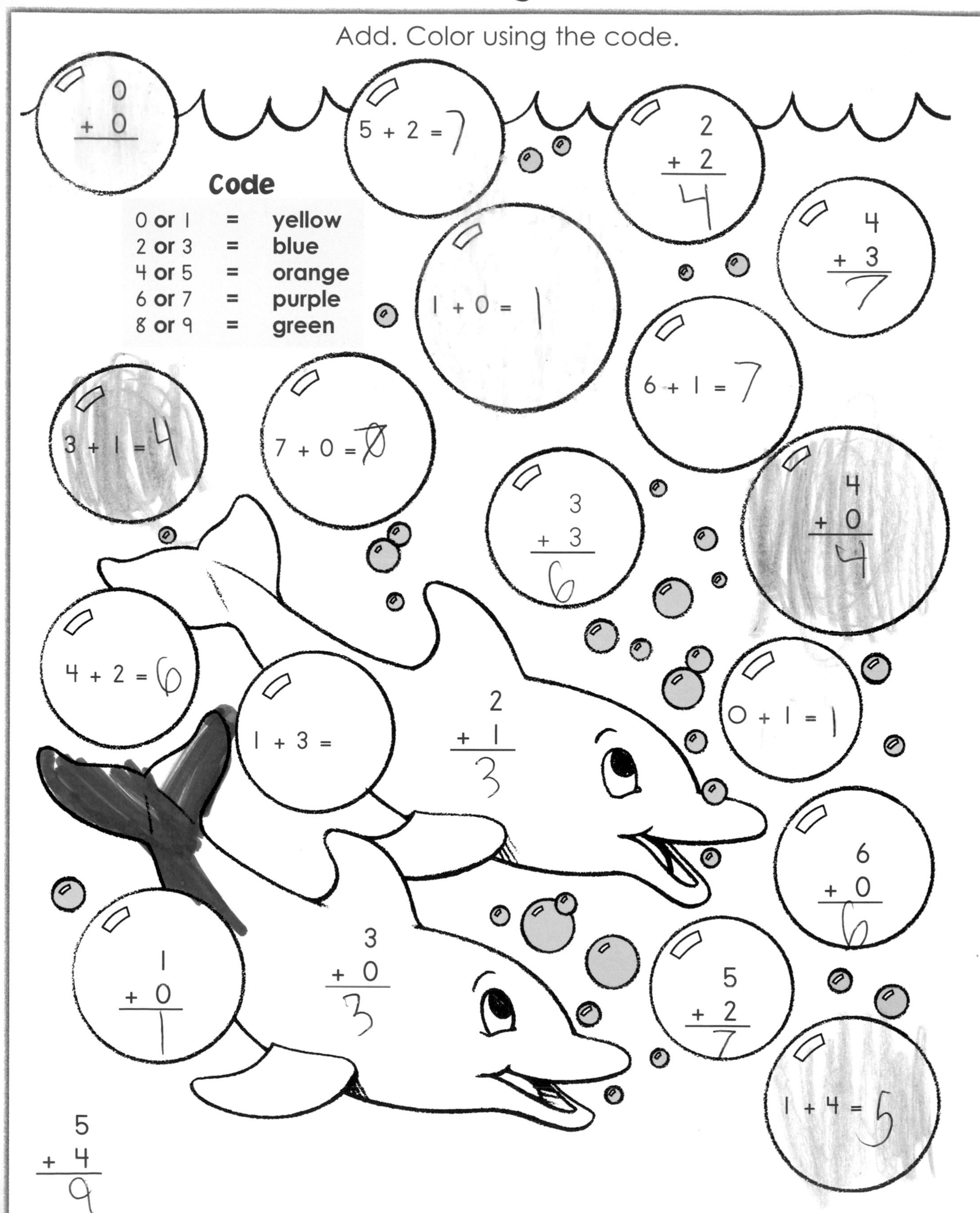

Code
0 or 1 = yellow
2 or 3 = blue
4 or 5 = orange
6 or 7 = purple
8 or 9 = green
0 + 0
5 + 2 =
2 + 2
4 + 3
1 + 0 =
6 + 1 =
3 + 1 =
7 + 0 =
3 + 3
4 + 0
4 + 2 =
1 + 3 =
2 + 1
0 + 1 =
6 + 0
1 + 0
3 + 0
5 + 2
1 + 4 =
5 + 4

# Capitalization

Capitalize the **first word in a sentence, days of the week, months,** and **proper names** of people and places.

**Example: W**e took **R**honda to **N**ew **Y**ork on a **F**riday in **J**une.

Circle the letters that need to be capitalized.

1. she played ball on our team.
2. dr. sharma is our dentist.
3. do you know paul brown?
4. we are going to atlanta in december.

5. may we go to the park on sunday?
6. on tuesday we can go swimming.
7. are you going with us on wednesday?
8. please call robin stuart tonight.
9. we are traveling to california on friday.
10. have you met my friend maria?
11. marsha and matthew are sister and brother.
12. our teacher this year is mr. perry.

# Yummy Good! (Addition to 10)

Add.

BRAIN BUILDER

How many honey pots have a sum less than 6? ______

# Short ĕ

Say the words. Listen to the short sound of the vowel **e**.

**wĕt**  **bĕll**  **nĕt** 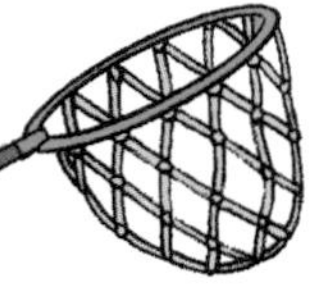

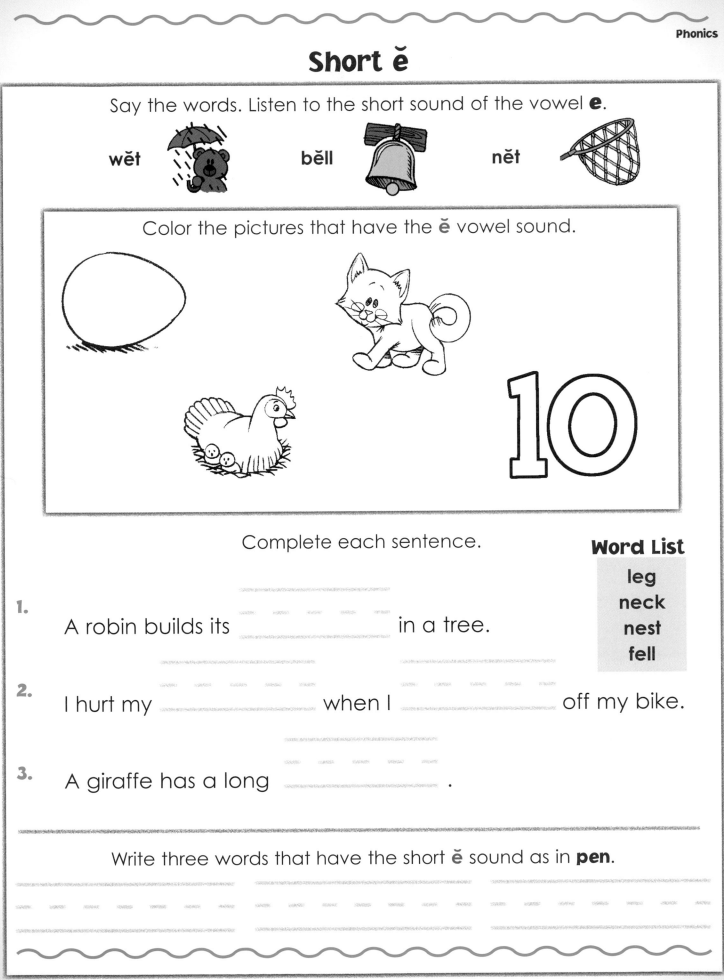

Color the pictures that have the ĕ vowel sound.

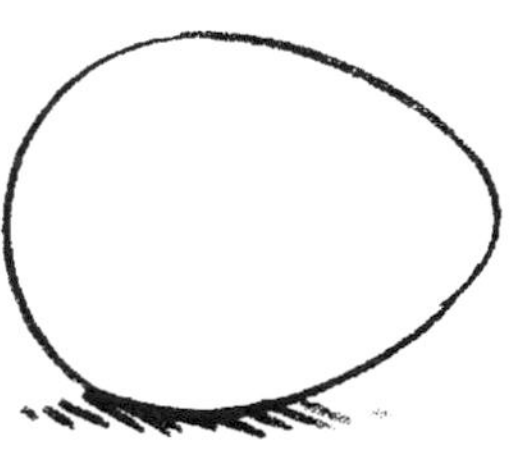

10

Complete each sentence.

**Word List**

- leg
- neck
- nest
- fell

1. A robin builds its ______________ in a tree.
2. I hurt my ______________ when I ______________ off my bike.
3. A giraffe has a long ______________ .

Write three words that have the short ĕ sound as in **pen**.

______________ ______________ ______________

# Short ĭ

Say the words. Listen to the short sound of the vowel **i**.

**sĭx**  **pĭg**  **lĭps** 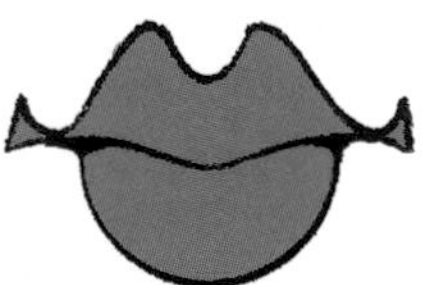

Color the pictures that have the ĭ vowel sound.

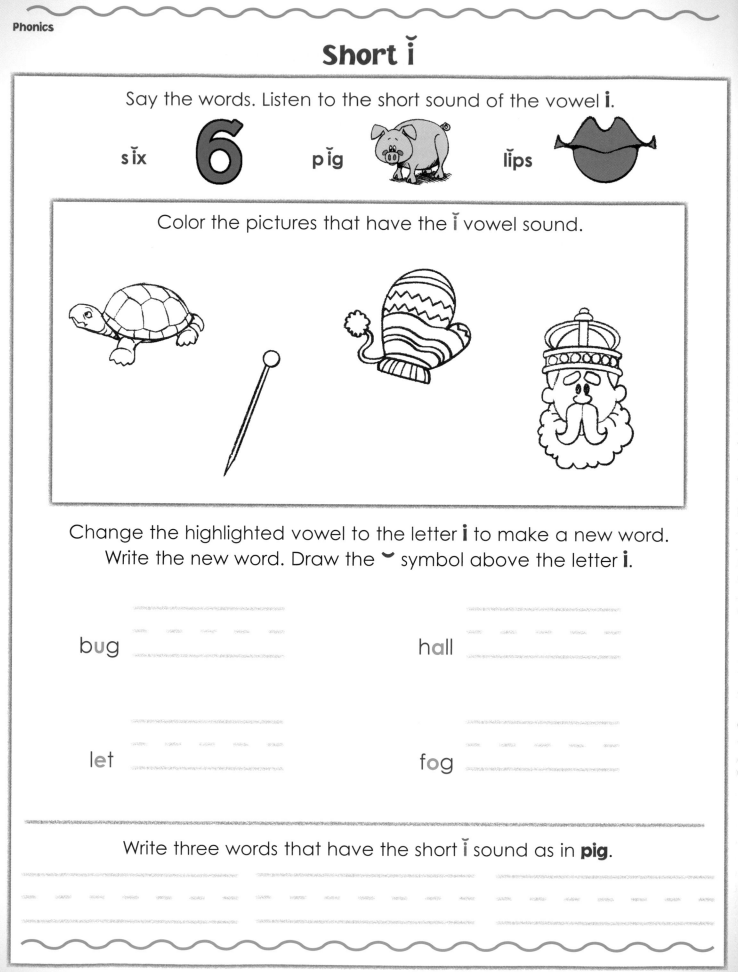

Change the highlighted vowel to the letter **i** to make a new word. Write the new word. Draw the ˘ symbol above the letter **i**.

bug ______________ hall ______________

let ______________ fog ______________

Write three words that have the short ĭ sound as in **pig**.

______________ ______________ ______________

# Addition Story Problems

**A.** Amy went to the museum.
She saw **5** dinosaurs in one room
and **3** dinosaurs in another room.
How many dinosaurs did Amy see in all?

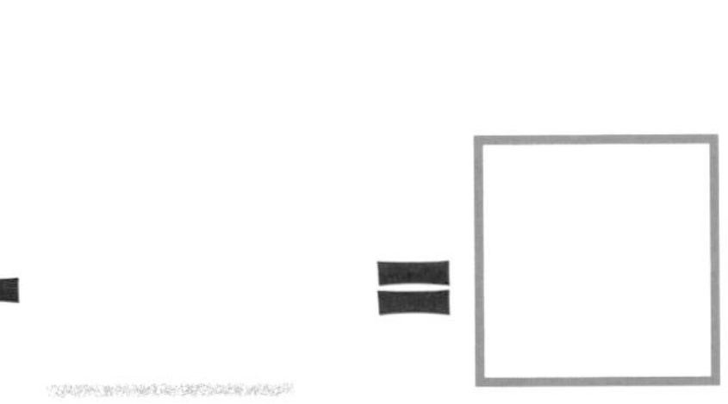

**B.** Stegasaurus laid **4** eggs.
Allosaurus laid **4** eggs, too.
What was the total number of eggs laid by the dinosaurs?

**C.** Put 12 counters in a row. Using your pencil, divide the counters into two sets. Start by putting your pencil after the first counter on the left, like this:

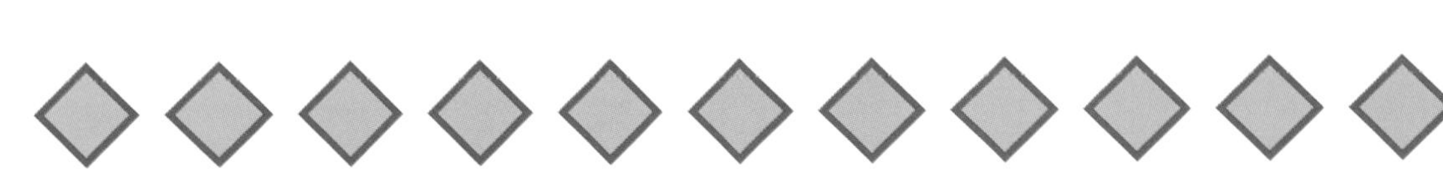

On another sheet of paper, write the combination you see (1 + 11).
Now move your pencil one counter to the right.
Write this combination under the first one you wrote.
Continue until you have moved your pencil all the way to the right.
Do you see any patterns?

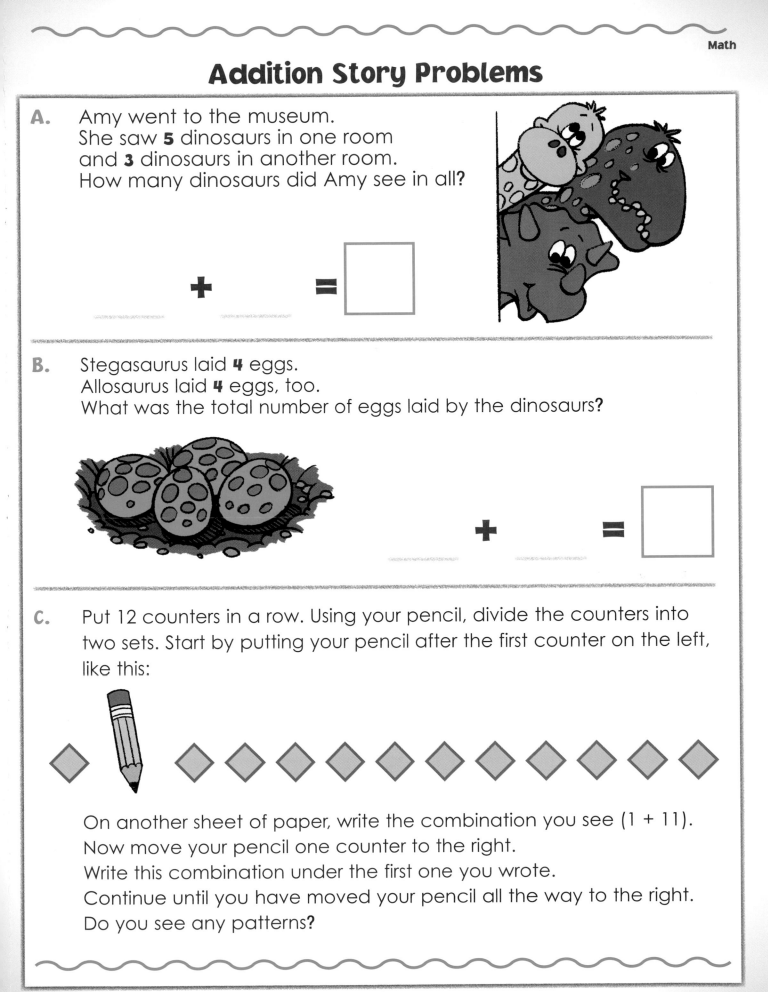

# Color the Farm

Say the name of everything you see in the picture.
Follow the directions.

1. Color the dog brown.
2. Color the pond blue.
3. Color the cow black.
4. Color the barn red.
5. Color the hen orange.
6. Color the tree green.

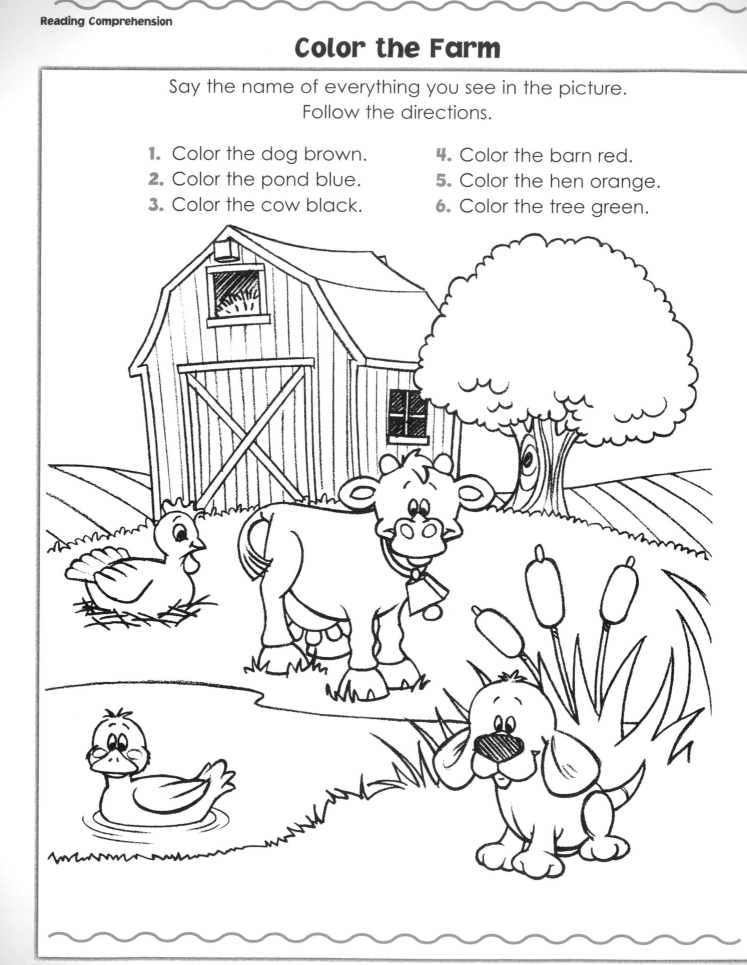

# Flying High! (Subtraction to 10)

Subtract. Color using the code. Then color the rest of the picture.

**Code**

**0 or 1 = blue**
**2 or 3 = yellow**

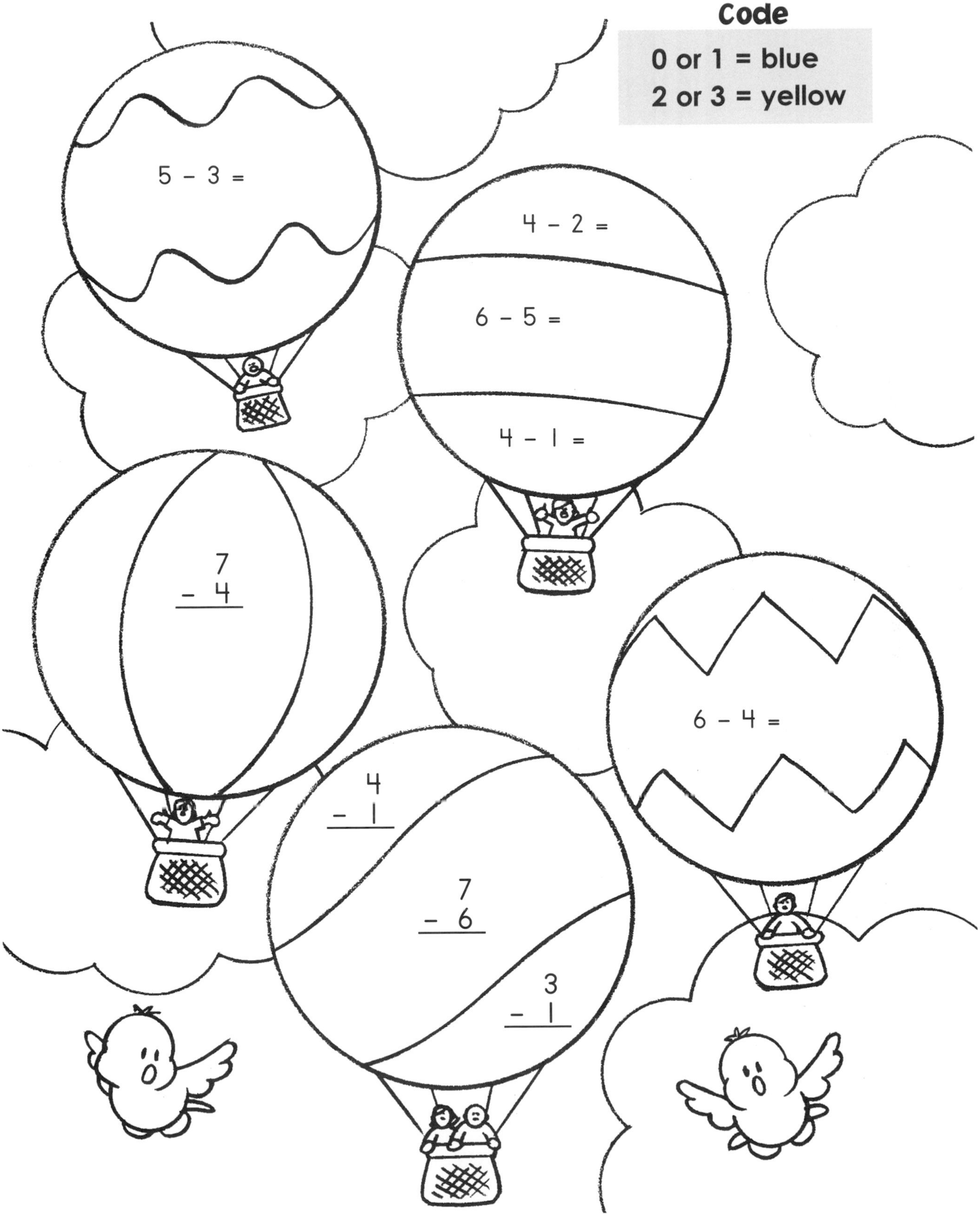

5 − 3 =

4 − 2 =

6 − 5 =

4 − 1 =

$$\begin{array}{r} 7 \\ -\ 4 \\ \hline \end{array}$$

6 − 4 =

$$\begin{array}{r} 4 \\ -\ 1 \\ \hline \end{array}$$

$$\begin{array}{r} 7 \\ -\ 6 \\ \hline \end{array}$$

$$\begin{array}{r} 3 \\ -\ 1 \\ \hline \end{array}$$

# Verbs (Action Words)

A **verb** is a word that shows action.

**Examples:** walk — I **walk** to school every day.
ride — My friend **rides** the bus.

Write the **verb** from the word list that matches each picture.

**Word List**

- drive
- cook
- eat
- sew
- swim
- run

Finish each sentence with a **verb** from the word list.

1. Mr. Henry ______________ hard on his farm.
2. He ______________ all the hungry pigs.
3. He ______________ corn and oats.
4. He ______________ the cows two times each day.

**Word List**

- milks
- works
- plants
- feeds

# Number Sentence Story Problems

Write a number sentence for each story problem.

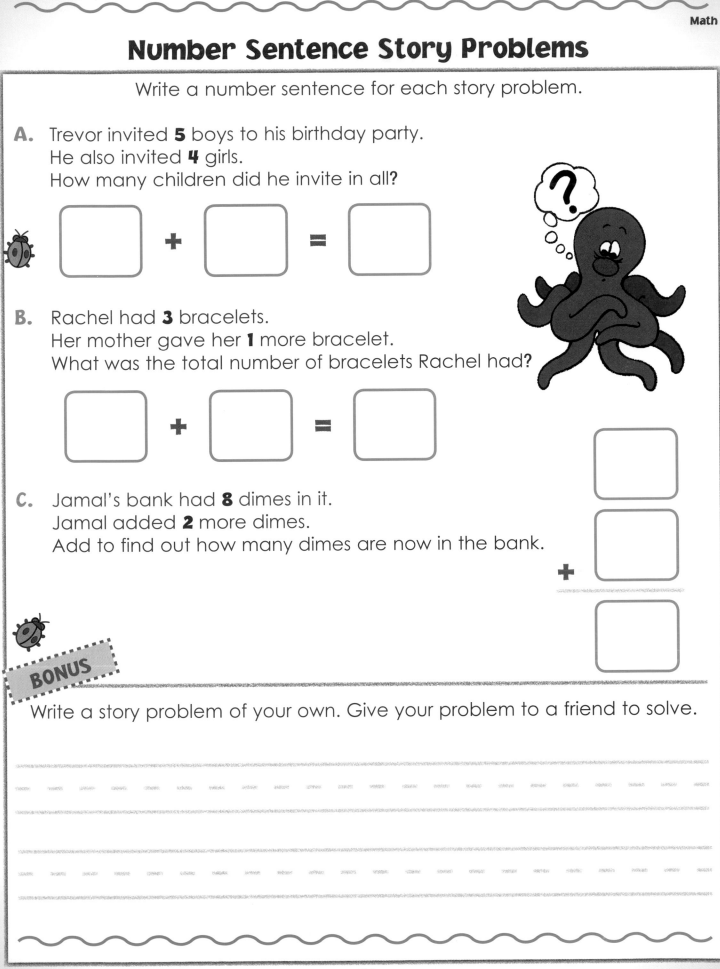

**A.** Trevor invited **5** boys to his birthday party.
He also invited **4** girls.
How many children did he invite in all?

☐ + ☐ = ☐

**B.** Rachel had **3** bracelets.
Her mother gave her **1** more bracelet.
What was the total number of bracelets Rachel had?

☐ + ☐ = ☐

**C.** Jamal's bank had **8** dimes in it.
Jamal added **2** more dimes.
Add to find out how many dimes are now in the bank.

☐
\+ ☐
☐

**BONUS**

Write a story problem of your own. Give your problem to a friend to solve.

# Adjectives (Describing Words)

An **adjective** is a word used to describe a noun.

**Example:** the **red** balloon

**A.** Circle the adjectives.

1. the big shoe
2. a tiny pebble
3. the loud radio
4. the colorful dress
5. the yellow bananas
6. a fuzzy puppy
7. the three elephants
8. a chewy taffy
9. a sour lemon
10. the two cupcakes

**B.** Write an adjective on the blank beside each noun.

1. ____________ dog
2. ____________ squirrel
3. ____________ carrots
4. ____________ daisy

1. ____________ bicycle
2. ____________ cowboy
3. ____________ monkey
4. ____________ seashell

# Pronouns

A **pronoun** is a word used in place of a noun.

**Example:** Elena is my cousin.
**She** is my cousin.

Choose the correct pronoun from the word list to replace the noun phrase in each ball. Write the pronoun on the blank.

**Word List**

- **he**
- **she**
- **it**
- **we**
- **they**

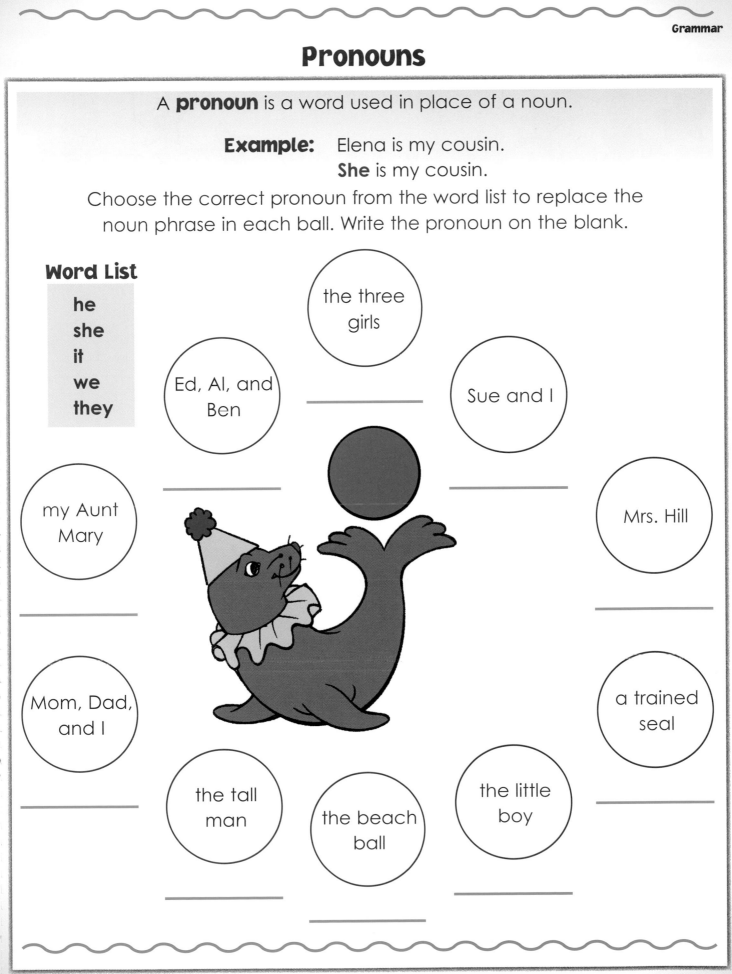

the three girls ________

Ed, Al, and Ben ________

Sue and I ________

my Aunt Mary ________

Mrs. Hill ________

Mom, Dad, and I ________

a trained seal ________

the tall man ________

the beach ball ________

the little boy ________

# Mixed Addition and Subtraction

Add or subtract.

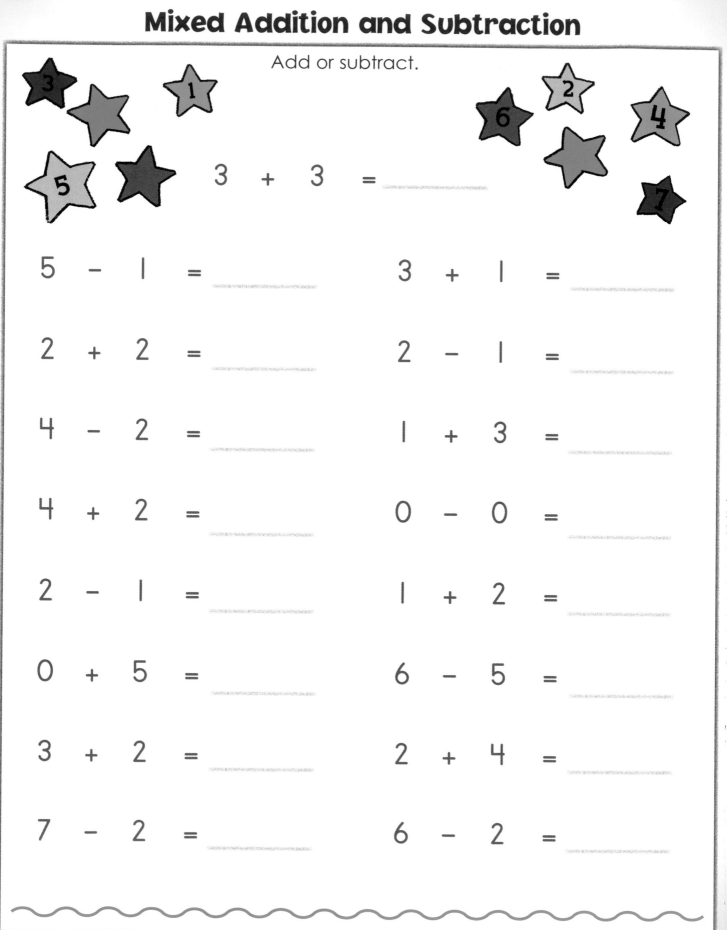

3 + 3 = ____

5 − 1 = ____ 3 + 1 = ____

2 + 2 = ____ 2 − 1 = ____

4 − 2 = ____ 1 + 3 = ____

4 + 2 = ____ 0 − 0 = ____

2 − 1 = ____ 1 + 2 = ____

0 + 5 = ____ 6 − 5 = ____

3 + 2 = ____ 2 + 4 = ____

7 − 2 = ____ 6 − 2 = ____

# Short ŏ

Say the words. Listen to the short sound of the vowel **o**.

**fŏx**  **lŏg** 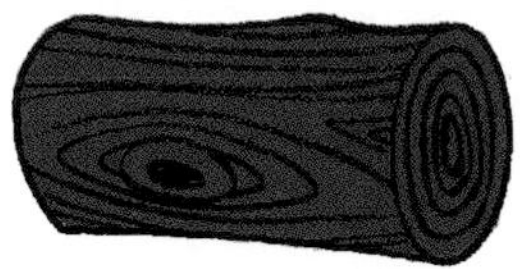 **clŏck** 

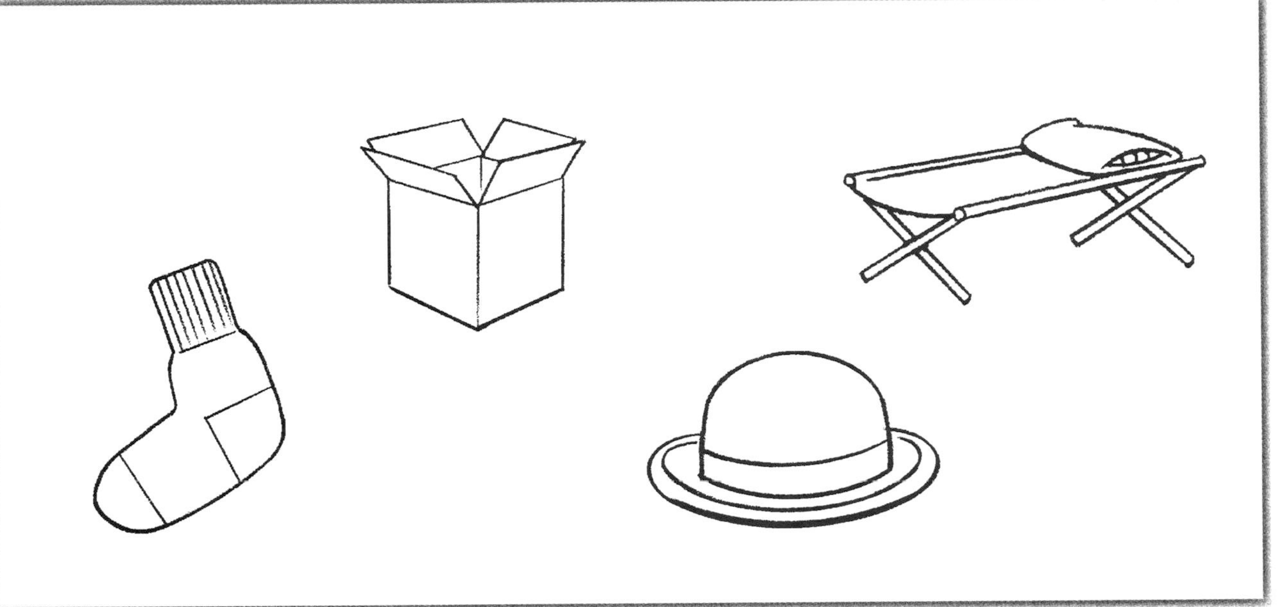

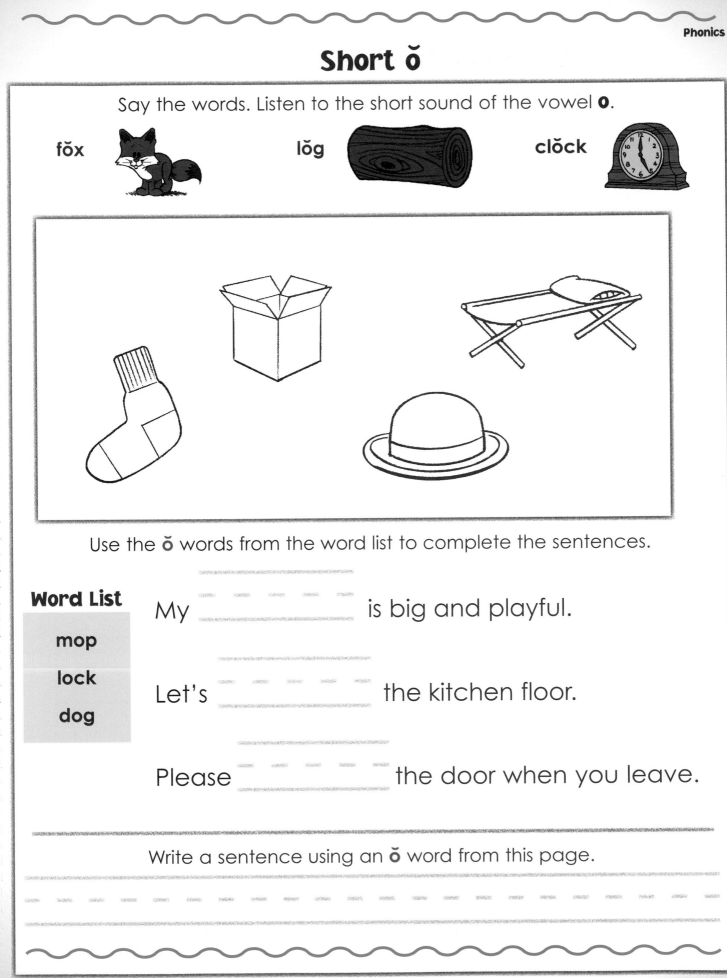

Use the ŏ words from the word list to complete the sentences.

**Word List**

- mop
- lock
- dog

My ________________ is big and playful.

Let's ________________ the kitchen floor.

Please ________________ the door when you leave.

Write a sentence using an ŏ word from this page.

________________________________________________

# Creating and Reading Graphs

Ask seven friends which sport they like best.
In the box below, make a tally mark beside the sport each one likes. Count the tally marks and color in the graph.

| | | |
|---|---|---|
| Baseball | | |
| Basketball | | |
| Football | | |
| Soccer | | |

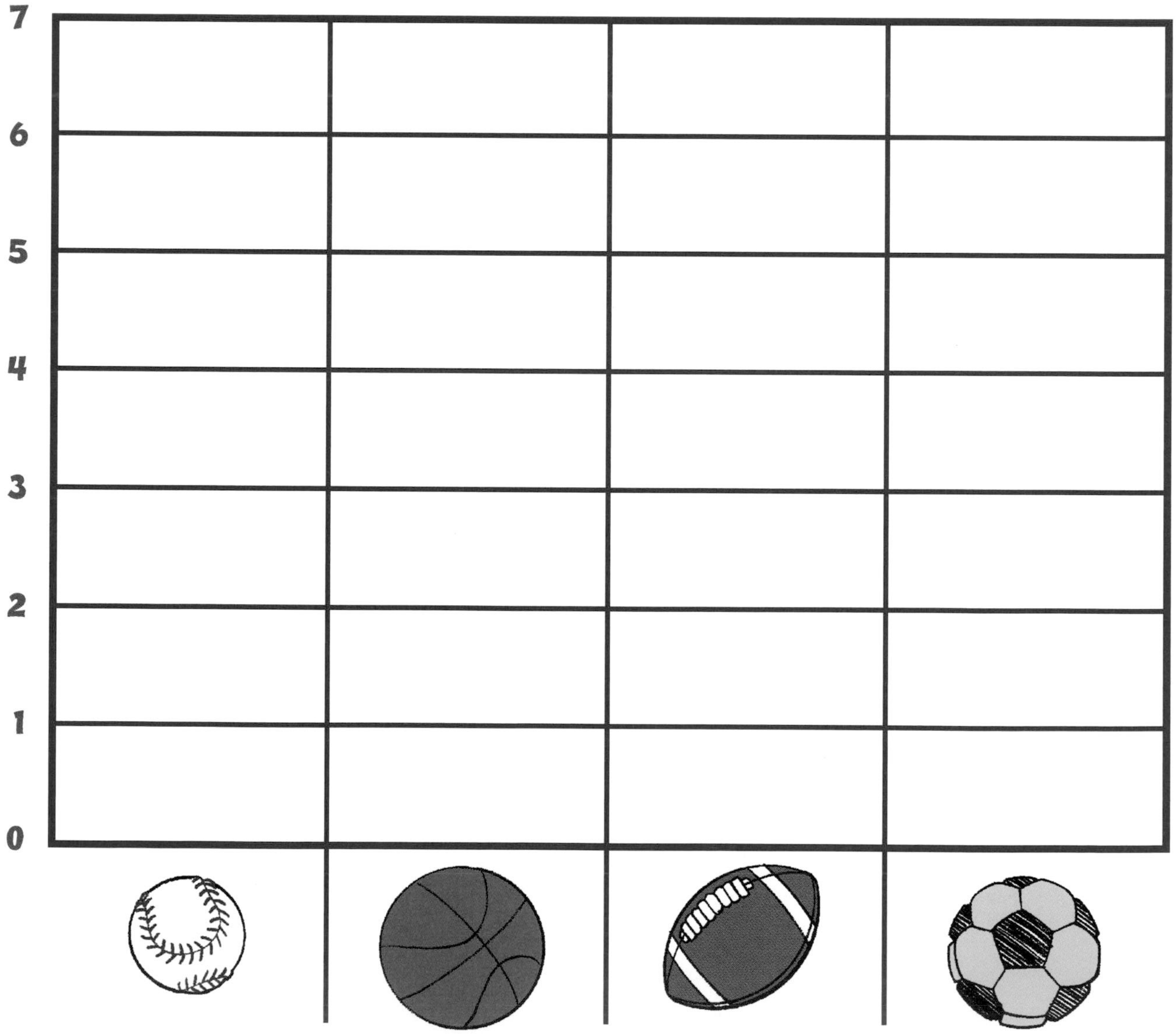

| | | | | |
|---|---|---|---|---|
| 7 | | | | |
| 6 | | | | |
| 5 | | | | |
| 4 | | | | |
| 3 | | | | |
| 2 | | | | |
| 1 | | | | |
| 0 | | | | |

# Singular and Plural Nouns

A noun that names one thing is called **singular**.
**Examples: book, tree**

A noun that names more than one thing is called **plural**.
Most words need only **s** to make them plural.
**Examples: books, trees**

Some words need **es** to make them plural. If a word ends with **s**, **ss**, **x**, **sh**, or **ch**, add **es** to the end of the word to make it plural.
**Examples: classes, churches**

Circle the correct plural word.

We had to buy (**nails  nailes**) at the store.

Put the (**boxs  boxes**) in the garage.

The (**dishs  dishes**) in the sink are dirty.

We got new (**dresss  dresses**) today.

The (**cooks  cookes**) at this restaurant are very good.

Jerome made three (**wishs  wishes**) on his birthday.

# Ordinal Numbers

Use the picture below to help you match the animals in each row with the words that show their places in line.

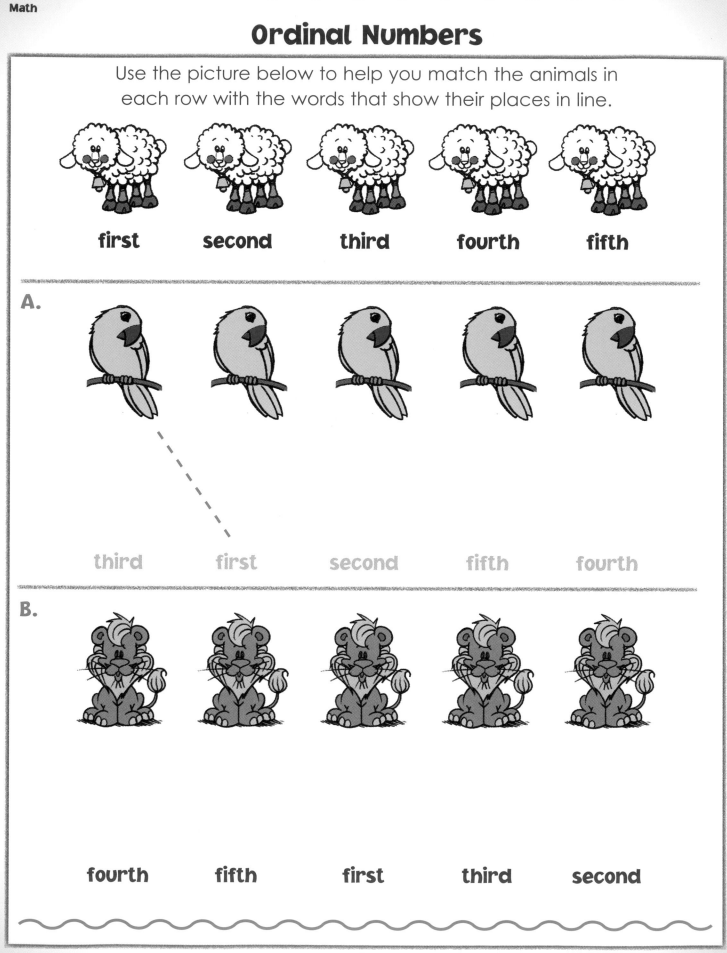

**first** **second** **third** **fourth** **fifth**

**A.**

third first second fifth fourth

**B.**

**fourth** **fifth** **first** **third** **second**

# Plural Nouns (-s, -es)

Read each word. Write **s** or **es** to make the word plural.

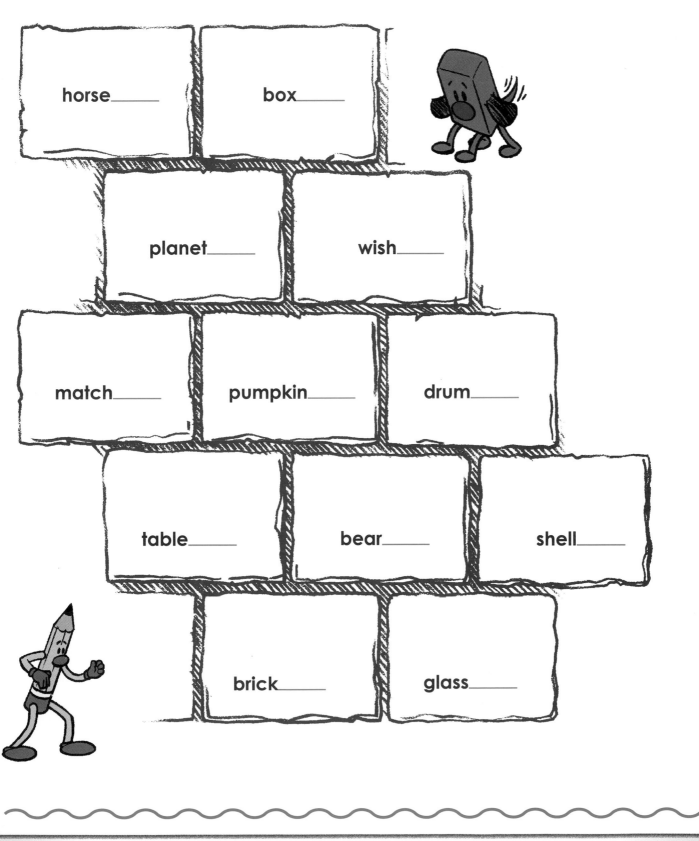

horse_____

box_____

planet_____

wish_____

match_____

pumpkin_____

drum_____

table_____

bear_____

shell_____

brick_____

glass_____

# Adding Numbers to 20

Complete each problem by writing the sum.

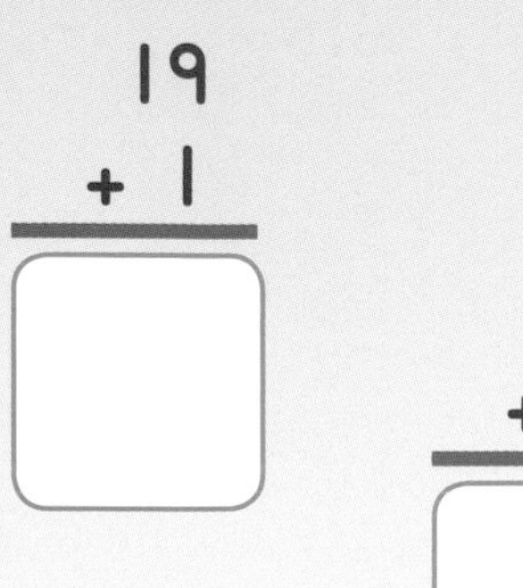

$$\begin{array}{r} 19 \\ +\ 1 \\ \hline \end{array}$$

$$\begin{array}{r} 9 \\ +\ 5 \\ \hline \end{array}$$

$$\begin{array}{r} 8 \\ +\ 7 \\ \hline \end{array}$$

$$\begin{array}{r} 6 \\ +\ 6 \\ \hline \end{array}$$

$$\begin{array}{r} 9 \\ +\ 2 \\ \hline \end{array}$$

$$\begin{array}{r} 20 \\ +\ 0 \\ \hline \end{array}$$

7 + 5 = ☐    4 + 8 = ☐    7 + 9 = ☐

Circle the number sentence in each pair that shows the correct sum.

| | | |
|---|---|---|
| 9 + 2 = 11 | 7 + 9 = 15 | 0 + 20 = 20 |
| 9 + 4 = 11 | 7 + 8 =-15 | 0 + 18 = 20 |

Write a number sentence that shows the numbers 8 and 6 added together.

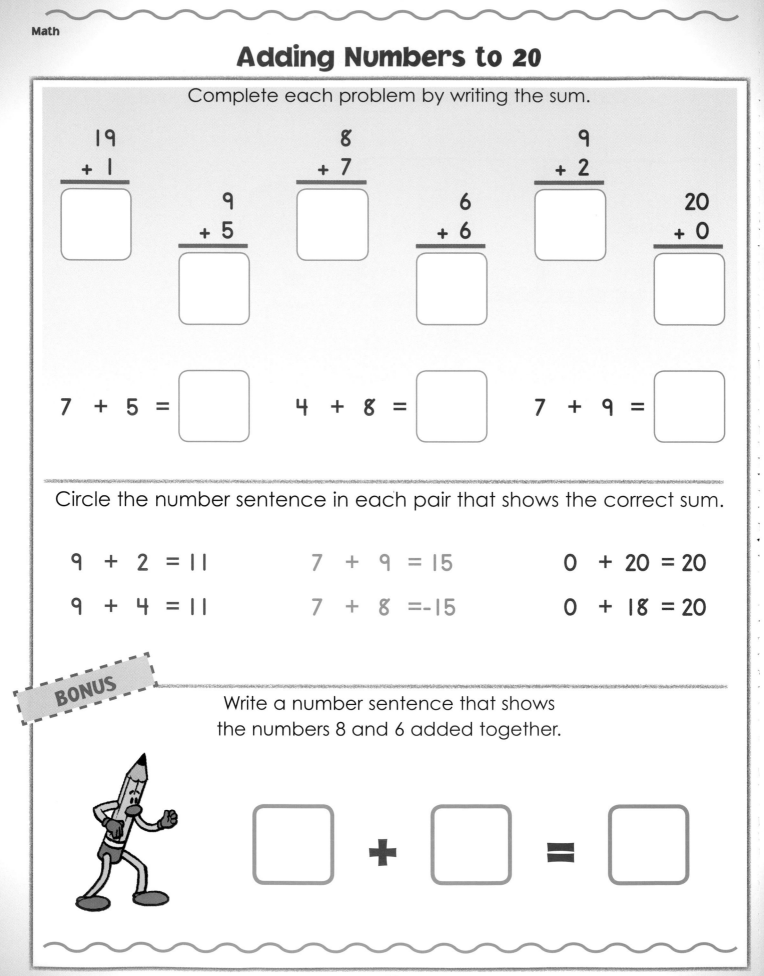

# Past Tense Verbs (-ed)

A **verb** can tell what is happening now or what has already happened (past). Most verbs add **ed** to tell the **past tense**.

| **Examples:** | **Now** | **jump** | I **jump** rope at recess. |
|---|---|---|---|
| | **Past** | **jumped** | I **jumped** rope yesterday. |

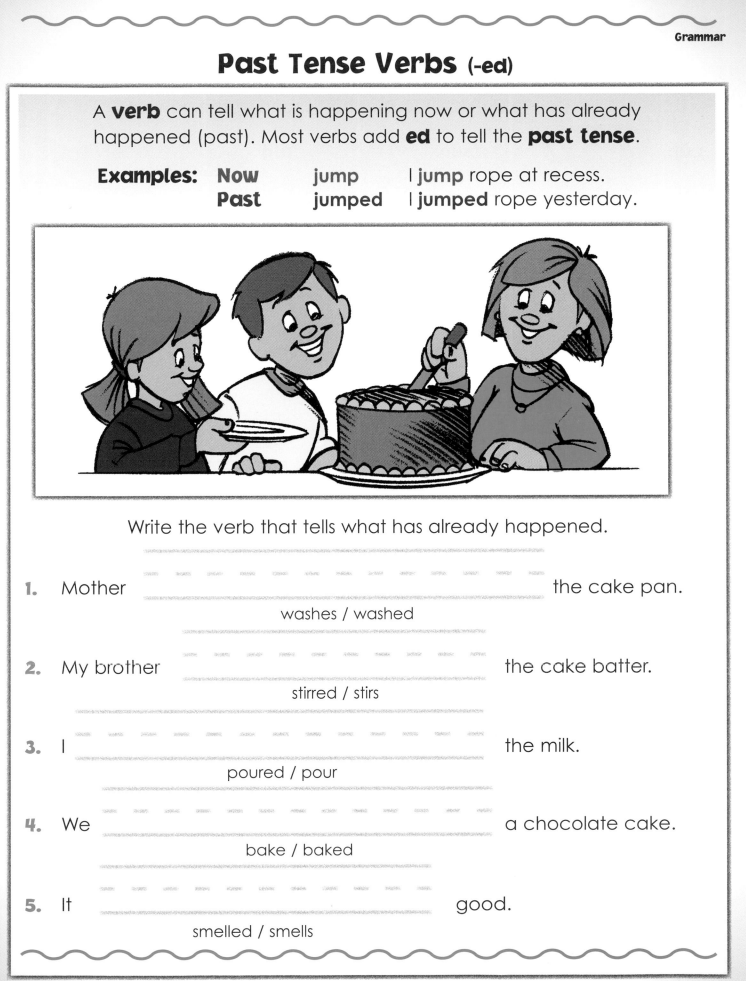

Write the verb that tells what has already happened.

**1.** Mother ________________ the cake pan.
washes / washed

**2.** My brother ________________ the cake batter.
stirred / stirs

**3.** I ________________ the milk.
poured / pour

**4.** We ________________ a chocolate cake.
bake / baked

**5.** It ________________ good.
smelled / smells

# Short ŭ

Say the words. Listen to the short sound of the vowel **u**.

**cŭp**  **sŭn**  **rŭg** 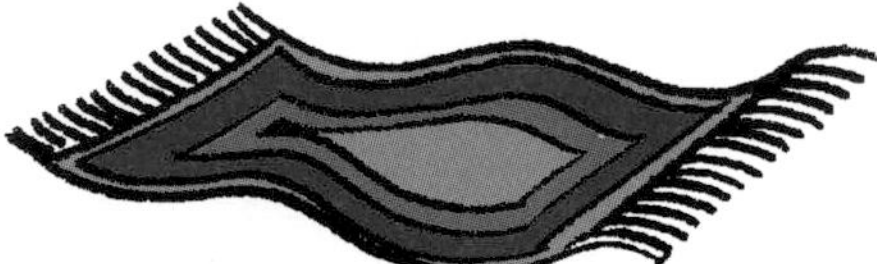

Color the pictures that have the **ŭ** vowel sound.

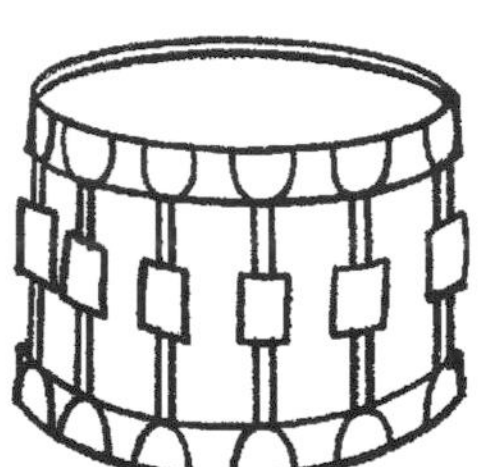

Read the words. Write each word next to the correct picture.

**Word List** **nut** **duck** **bug** **jug**

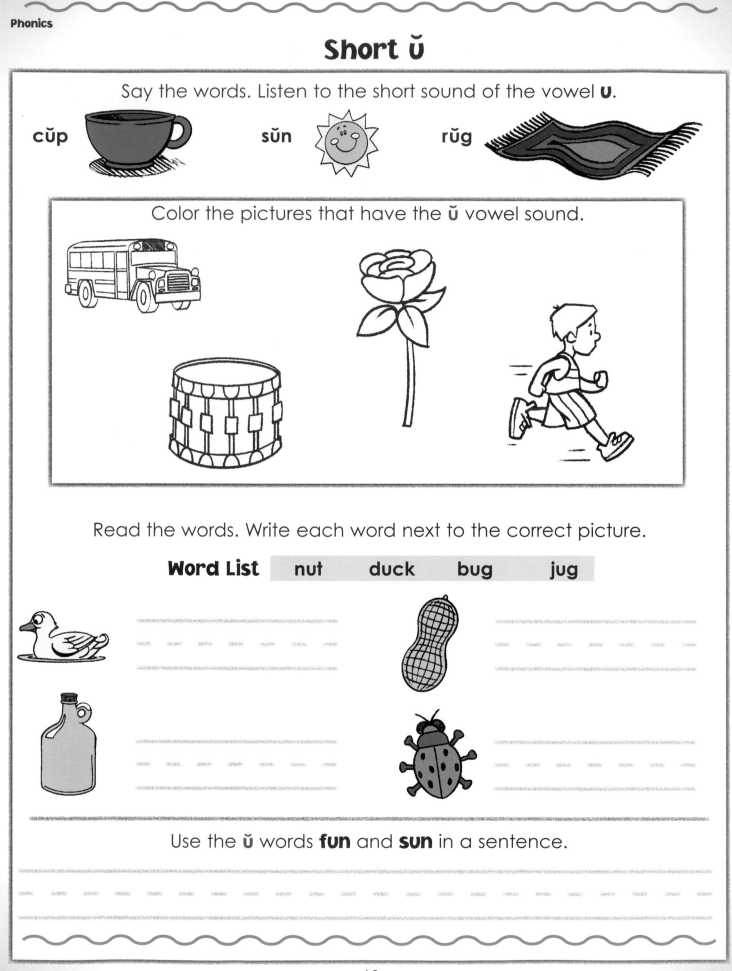

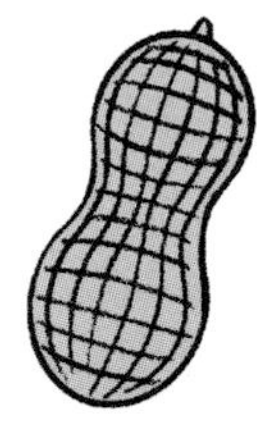

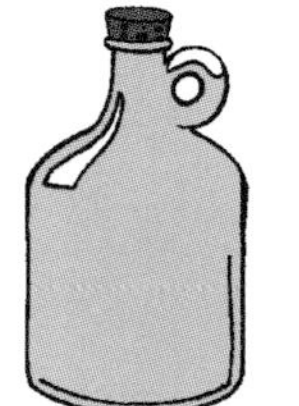

Use the **ŭ** words **fun** and **sun** in a sentence.

# Story Problems

Write a number sentence to solve each story problem.

**Example:** David wrote **14** letters.
Terry wrote **5** letters.
How many letters did they write altogether?

| 14 | + | 5 | = | 19 |
|---|---|---|---|---|
| (number of letters David wrote) | | (number of letters Terry wrote) | | (total number of letters written) |

**A.** Anthony held **7** rocks in one hand.
He held **9** rocks in his other hand.
What was the total number of rocks he held?

**B.** Larry had **8** clear marbles.
He had **6** colored marbles.
How many marbles did Larry have in all?

**C.** Sherri ate **20** strawberries.
Carmen ate **0** strawberries.
How many strawberries did the girls eat altogether?

Make up a story problem for the number sentence **4 + 8 = 12**.

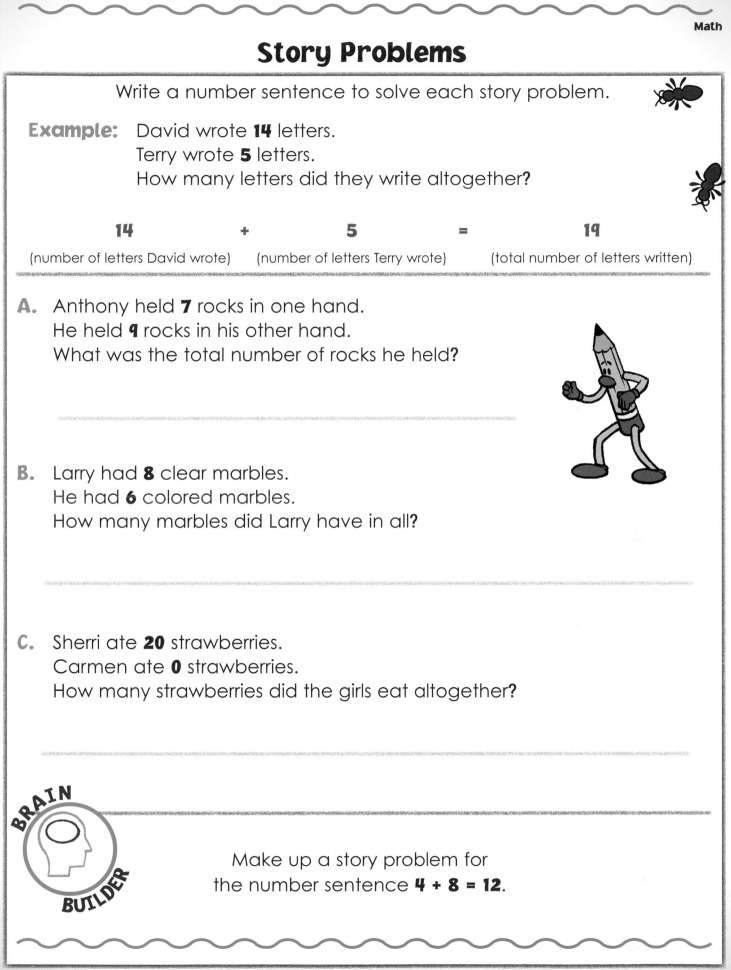

# Sentence Completion

Complete each sentence to make sense.

1. My friend ______________________________ .

2. Will you ______________________________ ?

3. I want ______________________________ .

4. She went ______________________________ .

5. The dogs ______________________________ .

# Subtraction to 18

Subtract.

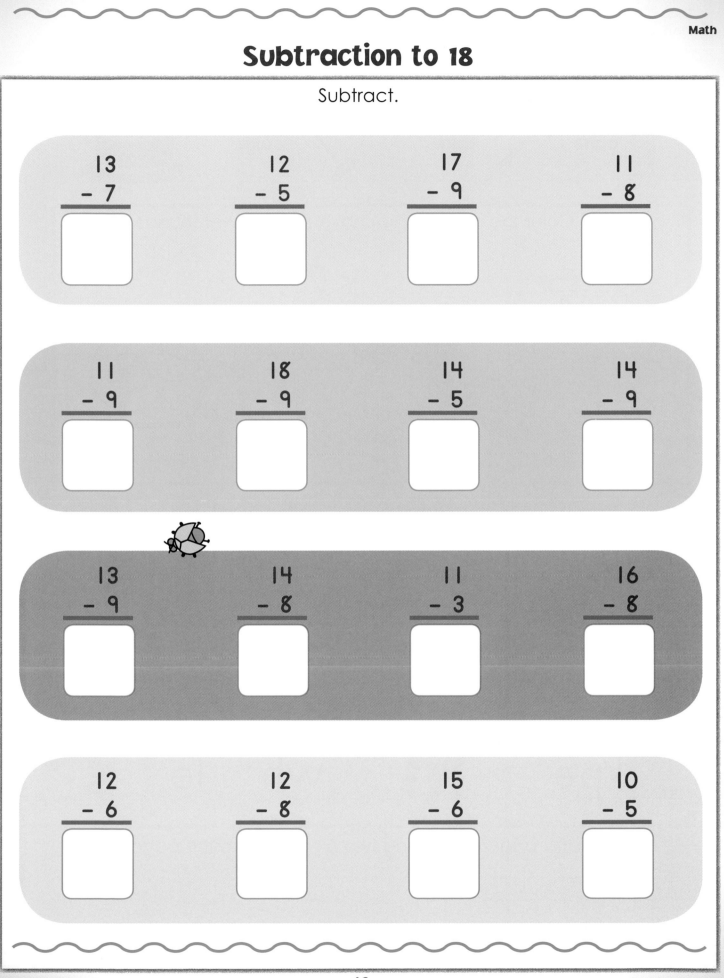

| | | | |
|---|---|---|---|
| 13 − 7 = ☐ | 12 − 5 = ☐ | 17 − 9 = ☐ | 11 − 8 = ☐ |
| 11 − 9 = ☐ | 18 − 9 = ☐ | 14 − 5 = ☐ | 14 − 9 = ☐ |
| 13 − 9 = ☐ | 14 − 8 = ☐ | 11 − 3 = ☐ | 16 − 8 = ☐ |
| 12 − 6 = ☐ | 12 − 8 = ☐ | 15 − 6 = ☐ | 10 − 5 = ☐ |

# Long ā

Say the words. Listen to the long sound of the vowel **a**.

**cāne**  **rāke**  **cāke** 

Color the pictures that have the **ā** vowel sound.

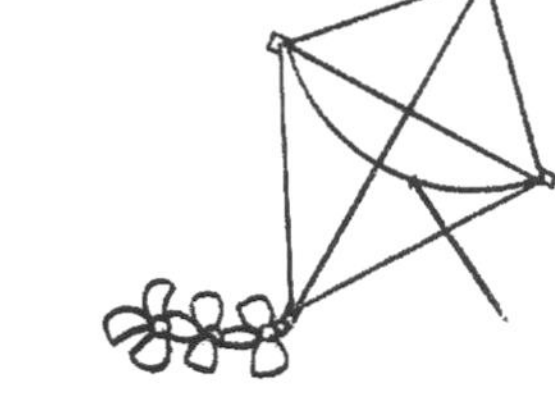
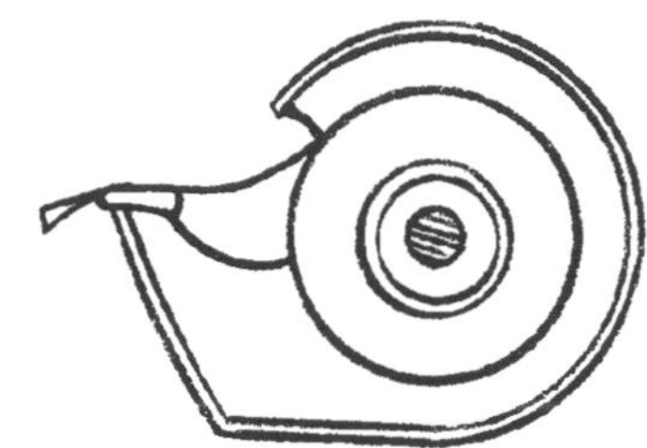

Write the letter **a** in each blank. Say the word and listen for the long vowel sound. Draw the ¯ symbol over the letter **a**.

g __ te  pl __ te 

pl __ ne  c __ pe 

__ pe  wh __ le 

Write a sentence using two **ā** words from this page.

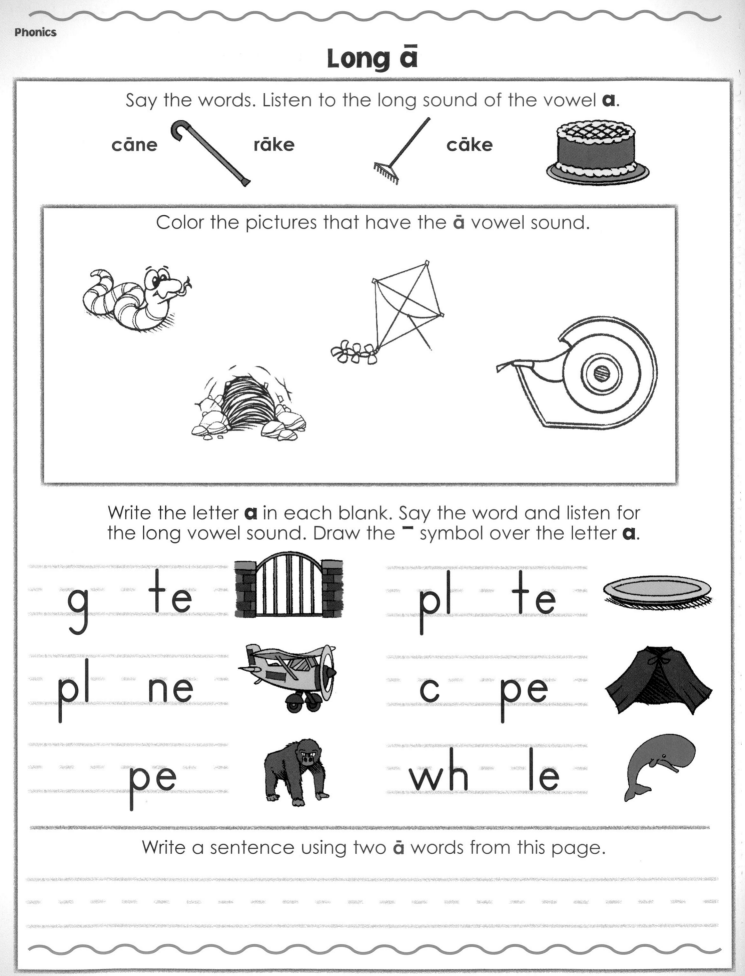

Cut and paste these words in "My Big Book of Words," found on pages 67–70. Put them in alphabetical order.

(Write your own words.)

| | | | | |
|---|---|---|---|---|
| ant | get | make | stop | |
| apple | goat | maybe | swim | |
| ball | gone | mine | tent | |
| balloon | happy | nest | there | |
| can | have | nose | under | |
| cat | hide | on | up | |
| come | inside | open | vase | |
| dark | it | pig | very | |
| dig | joke | play | wagon | |
| dog | jump | pretty | want | |
| eat | key | quill | work | |
| egg | kite | quit | xylophone | |
| end | kitten | rabbit | yak | |
| fish | lamp | red | yellow | |
| four | like | run | zipper | |
| fox | look | said | zoo | |

Remove pages 67–70. Cut along dashed lines. Staple pages in order.

# My Big Book of Words

Write in your own words or use the "cut-and-paste" words found on page 65. Put the words in alphabetical order.

1

| Ee | Ff | Gg | Hh |
| --- | --- | --- | --- |
| | | | |

3

| Aa | Bb | Cc | Dd |
|---|---|---|---|
| | | | |

2

| Ii | Jj | Kk | Ll |
|---|---|---|---|
| | | | |

4

| Mm | Nn | Oo | Pp |
| --- | --- | --- | --- |
| | | | |

5

| Uu | Vv | Ww | Xx |
| --- | --- | --- | --- |
| | | | |

7

| Qq | Rr | Ss | Tt |
| --- | --- | --- | --- |
| | | | |

6

| Yy | Zz | My Favorite Words |
| --- | --- | --- |
| | | |

8

# Fact Families

A **fact family** is a group of addition and subtraction number sentences that have the same three numbers.

| | |
|---|---|
| 9 + 8 = 17 | 17 - 9 = 8 |
| 8 + 9 = 17 | 17 - 8 = 9 |

The numbers 8, 9, and 17 are used in the **fact family** above.

Complete each number sentence. Draw a line to match each pair of number sentences from the same fact family.

8 + 7 = ☐

9 + 3 = ☐

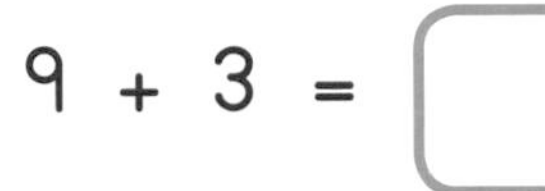

6 + 5 = ☐

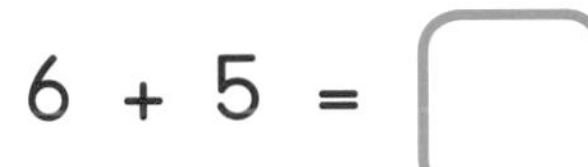

9 + 7 = ☐

3 + 9 = ☐

7 + 8 = ☐

7 + 9 = ☐

5 + 6 = ☐

Write two addition number sentences to complete each fact family. Use the same three numbers as in the subtraction number sentences.

11 - 5 = 6

11 - 6 = 5

☐ + ☐ = ☐

☐ + ☐ = ☐

14 - 6 = 8

14 - 8 = 6

☐ + ☐ = ☐

☐ + ☐ = ☐

# Rhyming Words

See how many words you can print that rhyme with **man**. First, try to add different letters to **-an** on your own. Use the letter box if you get stuck.

1.

2.

3.

4.

5.

6.

7.

8.

9.

**Letter Box**

b c D f
N p r t v

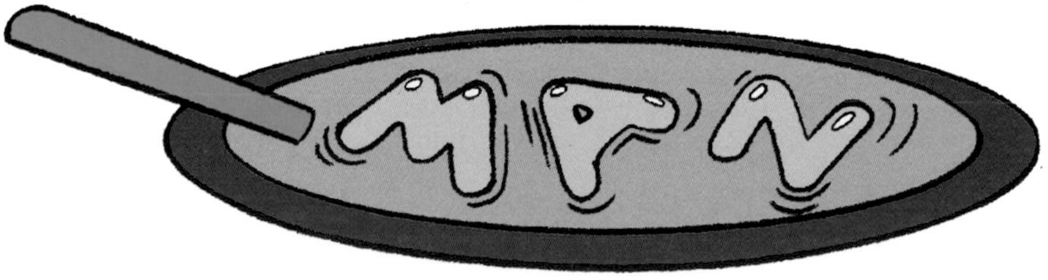

# Missing Addends

In some number sentences, an addend is missing.

**6 + ☐ = 13**

To solve, think . . . "6 plus **how many** equals 13?"

**6 + 7 = 13**

6 + ☐ = 12

7 + ☐ = 12

4 + ☐ = 13

19 + ☐ = 20

2 + ☐ = 11

5 + ☐ = 13

1 + ☐ = 15

8 + ☐ = 11

7 + ☐ = 14

3 + ☐ = 12

9 + ☐ = 18

Make up two problems of your own.

☐ + ☐ = **12**

☐ + ☐ = **10**

# Long ē

Say the words. Listen to the long sound of the vowel **e**.

**scēne** **thēse** **ēve**

Read each word in the word list.
Use the words to complete each sentence.
Draw the **–** symbol above the long vowel sound.

**Word List** **Steve** **even** **scene** **Eve**

1. The boy's name is ______________.

2. We watched the first ______________ of the play.

3. We have a special dinner on Christmas ______________.

4. The teacher asked me to name an ______________ number.

Write your own sentence using one **ē** word from the word list.

______________________________

# Doubles Facts

Sometimes a number is added to itself.
These number sentences are called **doubles facts**.

**5 + 5 = 10** **8 + 8 = 16**

Complete the doubles facts.

7 + 7 = ___

5 + ___ = 10

10 + 10 = ___

1 + ___ = 2

7 + ___ = 14

0 + 0 = ___

6 + 6 = ___

2 + ___ = 4

4 + 4 = ___

9 + ___ = 18

___ + 4 = 8

3 + 3 = ___

5 + 5 = ___

1 + 1 = ___

$$\begin{array}{r} \_\_\_ \\ +\ 3 \\ \hline 6 \end{array}$$

$$\begin{array}{r} 8 \\ +\ 8 \\ \hline \_\_\_ \end{array}$$

$$\begin{array}{r} \_\_\_ \\ +\ 6 \\ \hline 12 \end{array}$$

# Action Words

Complete each sentence.

**Word List**

| swing | jump | walk |
|---|---|---|
| run | ride | swim |

1. I like to ______________ my bike.

2. My sister loves to ______________ high.

3. Nick can ______________ like a frog.

4. At the pool, I like to ______________ .

5. Kelly can ______________ very fast.

# Rhyming Pairs

Fill in the blank with a word that rhymes with the word in color.

She likes to **run** under the ______________.

I see a **bee** up in the ______________.

He can **hop** over the ______________.

There is a **man** inside the ______________.

Make up a rhyme.
Draw a picture of your rhyme on another sheet of paper.

# Tens and Ones

Write the number that each drawing represents.

 ______

 ______

 ______

 ______

 ______

 ______

 ______

 ______

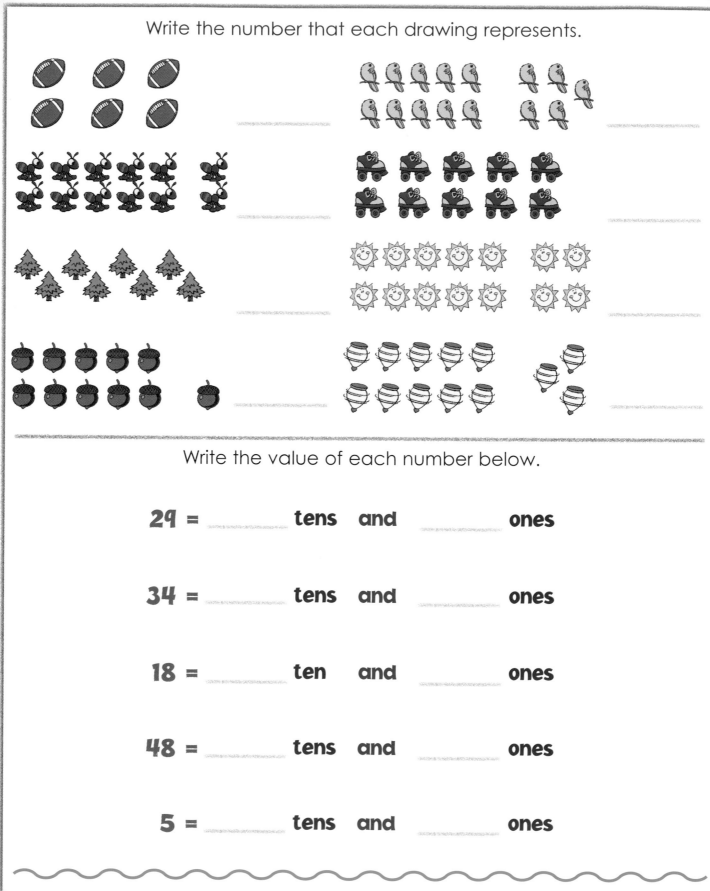

Write the value of each number below.

**29** = ______ **tens and** ______ **ones**

**34** = ______ **tens and** ______ **ones**

**18** = ______ **ten and** ______ **ones**

**48** = ______ **tens and** ______ **ones**

**5** = ______ **tens and** ______ **ones**

# Punctuation Marks

Write the correct **punctuation mark** at the end of each sentence. Put a **?** or **.** in each box.

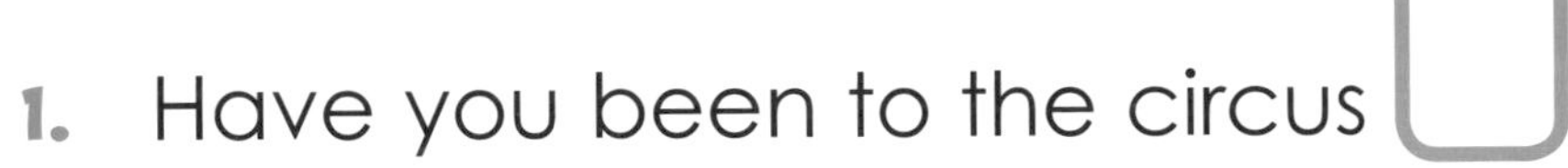

1. Have you been to the circus ☐

2. We went on Saturday ☐

3. We saw monkeys ☐

4. Would you like to be a clown ☐

5. We ate lots of fluffy, pink cotton candy ☐

6. Have you ever had a candy apple ☐

7. It is my favorite thing to eat ☐

# Place Value Practice

Write the number of tens and ones.

20 =

| tens | ones |
| --- | --- |
| | |

16 =

| tens | ones |
| --- | --- |
| | |

14 =

| tens | ones |
| --- | --- |
| | |

31 =

| tens | ones |
| --- | --- |
| | |

22 =

| tens | ones |
| --- | --- |
| | |

12 =

| tens | ones |
| --- | --- |
| | |

47 =

| tens | ones |
| --- | --- |
| | |

24 =

| tens | ones |
| --- | --- |
| | |

36 =

| tens | ones |
| --- | --- |
| | |

55 =

| tens | ones |
| --- | --- |
| | |

11 =

| tens | ones |
| --- | --- |
| | |

63 =

| tens | ones |
| --- | --- |
| | |

21 =

| tens | ones |
| --- | --- |
| | |

17 =

| tens | ones |
| --- | --- |
| | |

69 =

| tens | ones |
| --- | --- |
| | |

Add these numbers: **41, 26, 11**.
How many tens and ones
are in your answer?

| tens | ones |
| --- | --- |
| | |

# Long ī

Say the words. Listen to the long sound of the vowel **i**.

**kīte** 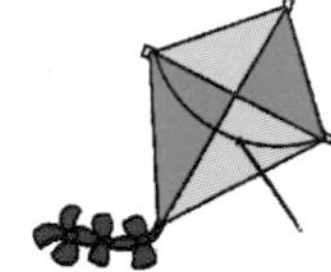 **tīre**  **fīre** 

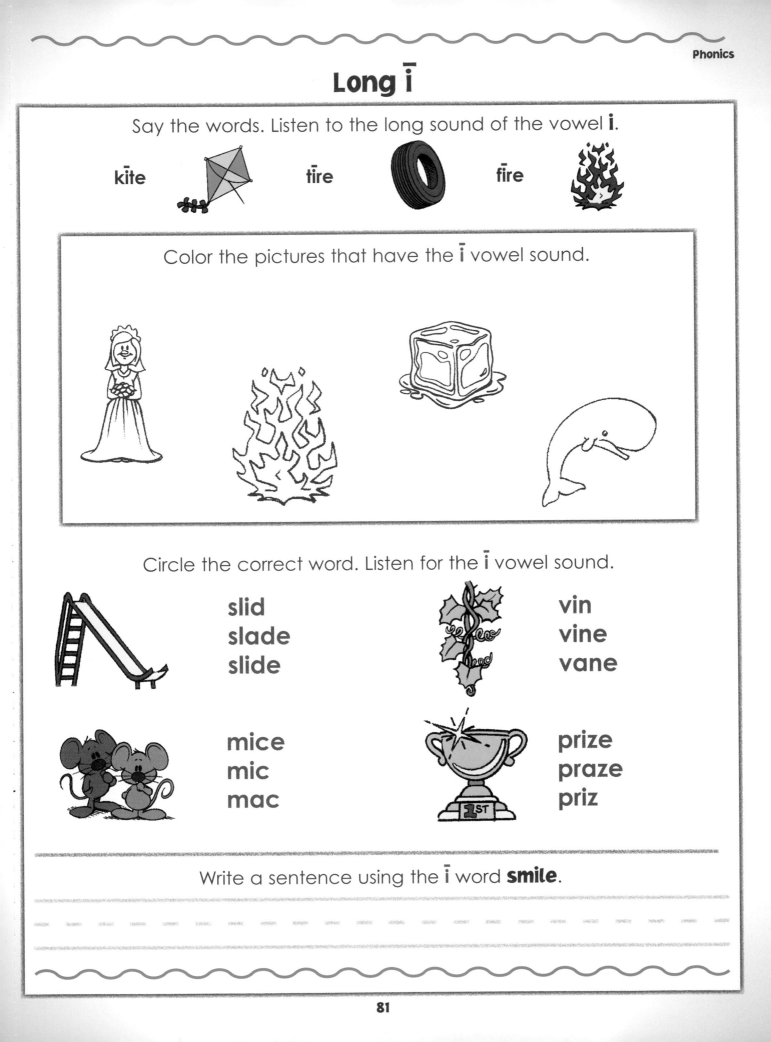

Color the pictures that have the ī vowel sound.

Circle the correct word. Listen for the ī vowel sound.

**slid**
**slade**
**slide**

**vin**
**vine**
**vane**

**mice**
**mic**
**mac**

**prize**
**praze**
**priz**

Write a sentence using the ī word **smile**.

# Compound Words

Write the two words that make up each compound word.

doghouse ______ + ______

football ______ + ______

fishbowl ______ ______

sandbox ______ + ______

rainbow ______ ______

suitcase ______ + ______

# Adding Two-Digit Numbers

Add the tens and ones to find the two-digit sum.

**2** tens and **6** ones
**+ 1** ten and **3** ones

3 tens and 9 ones = 39

**1** ten and **4** ones
**+ 3** tens and **3** ones

☐ tens and ☐ ones =

**1** ten and **3** ones
**+ 1** ten and **1** one

☐ tens and ☐ ones =

**2** tens and **5** ones
**+ 2** tens and **0** ones

☐ tens and ☐ ones =

**1** ten and **6** ones
**+ 2** tens and **3** ones

☐ tens and ☐ ones =

**1** ten and **4** ones
**+ 3** tens and **1** one

☐ tens and ☐ ones =

**1** ten and **5** ones
**+ 2** tens and **4** ones

☐ tens and ☐ ones =

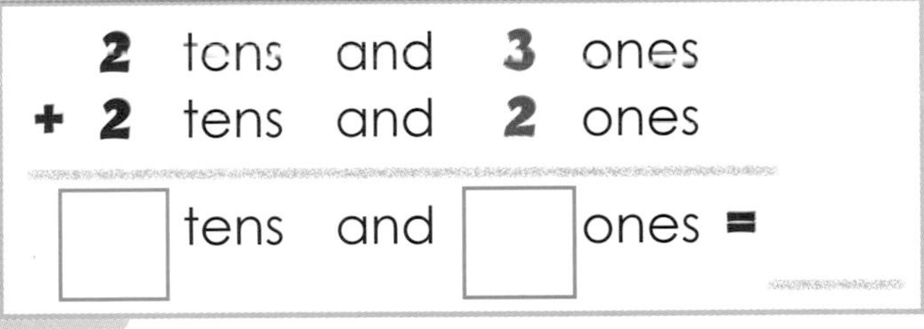

**2** tens and **3** ones
**+ 2** tens and **2** ones

☐ tens and ☐ ones =

**3** tens and **2** ones
**+ 1** ten and **1** one

☐ tens and ☐ ones =

**3** tens and **7** ones
**+ 1** ten and **2** ones

☐ tens and ☐ ones =

# Two Words in One

Write the two words that make each compound word.

# Double-Digit Addition

Add. Color the spaces with sums **greater** than 50 red.
Color the spaces with sums **less** than 50 blue.

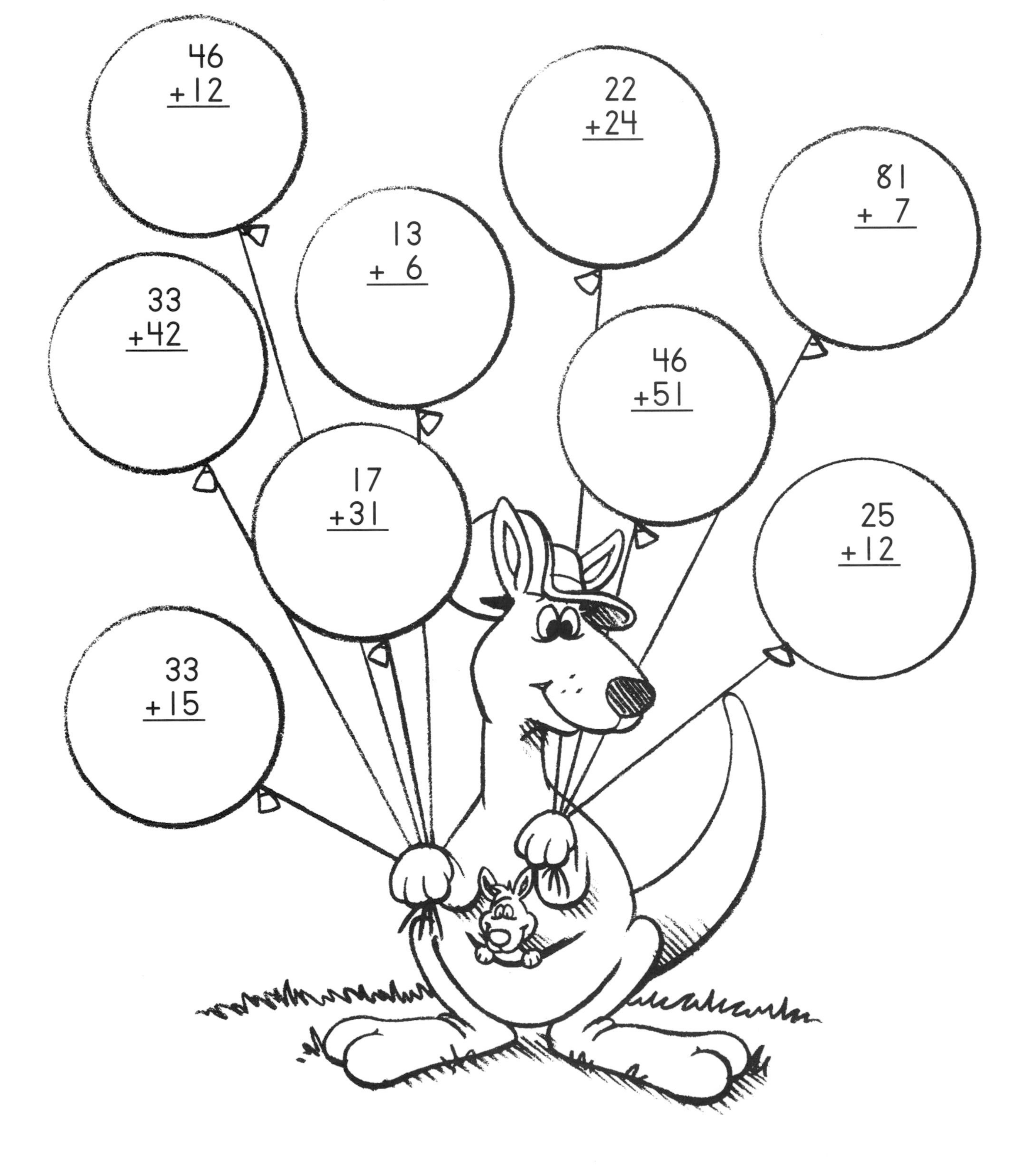

# Long ō

Say the words. Listen to the long sound of the vowel **o**.

**rōse**  **vōte**  **nōse** 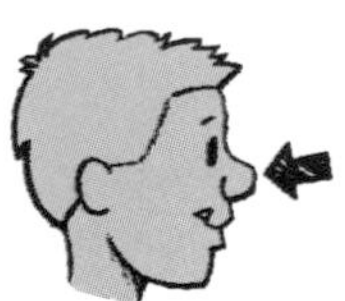

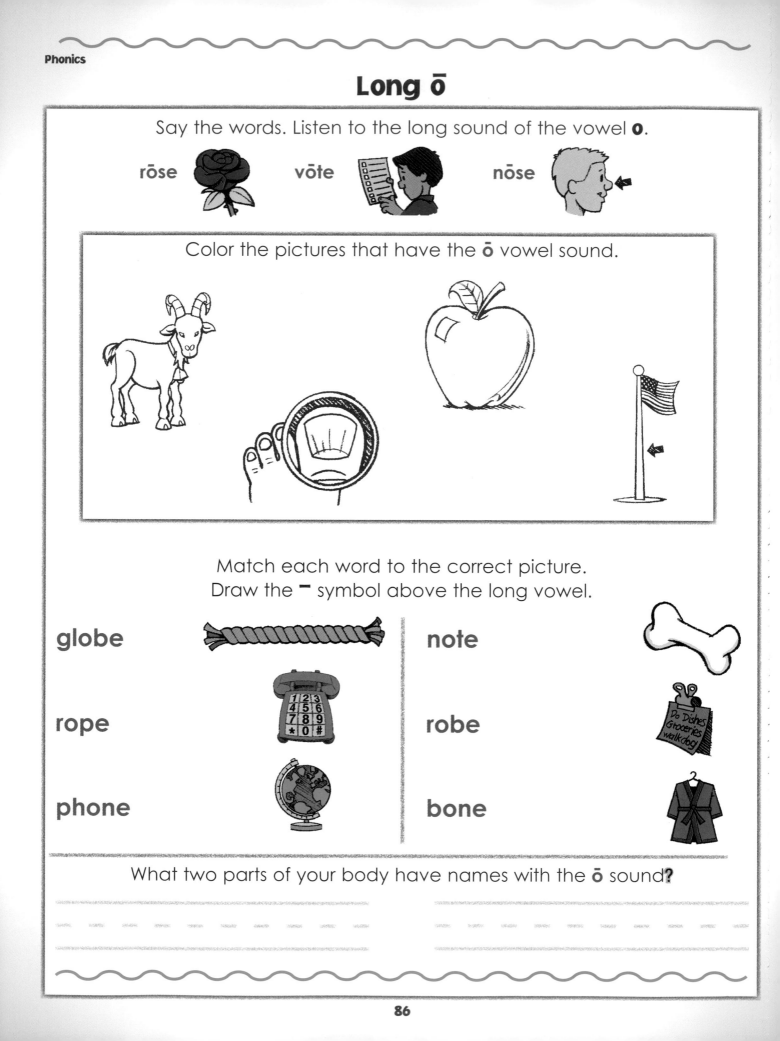

Color the pictures that have the **ō** vowel sound.

Match each word to the correct picture.
Draw the **¯** symbol above the long vowel.

**globe** 

**rope** 

**phone** 

**note** 

**robe** 

**bone** 

What two parts of your body have names with the **ō** sound?

# Connect the Sums

Add. Connect the equal sums. Color the picture.

$$\begin{array}{r} 12 \\ +\ 13 \\ \hline \end{array}$$

$$\begin{array}{r} 24 \\ +\ 15 \\ \hline \end{array}$$

$$\begin{array}{r} 32 \\ +\ 10 \\ \hline \end{array}$$

$$\begin{array}{r} 41 \\ +\ 17 \\ \hline \end{array}$$

$$\begin{array}{r} 26 \\ +\ 43 \\ \hline \end{array}$$

$$\begin{array}{r} 54 \\ +\ 33 \\ \hline \end{array}$$

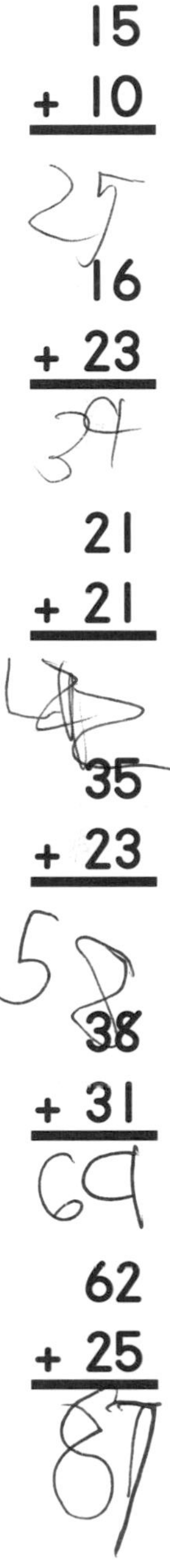

$$\begin{array}{r} 15 \\ +\ 10 \\ \hline \end{array}$$

$$\begin{array}{r} 16 \\ +\ 23 \\ \hline \end{array}$$

$$\begin{array}{r} 21 \\ +\ 21 \\ \hline \end{array}$$

$$\begin{array}{r} 35 \\ +\ 23 \\ \hline \end{array}$$

$$\begin{array}{r} 38 \\ +\ 31 \\ \hline \end{array}$$

$$\begin{array}{r} 62 \\ +\ 25 \\ \hline \end{array}$$

# Main Idea

Read the stories below.
Write the **main idea** of each story in the space provided.

Joe had a birthday party. He invited his friends. He got presents. He ate cake and ice cream.

Teena wore a costume. She went from house to house. People gave her candy. It was Halloween.

# Astro-Addition

Find the sums. Color the picture.

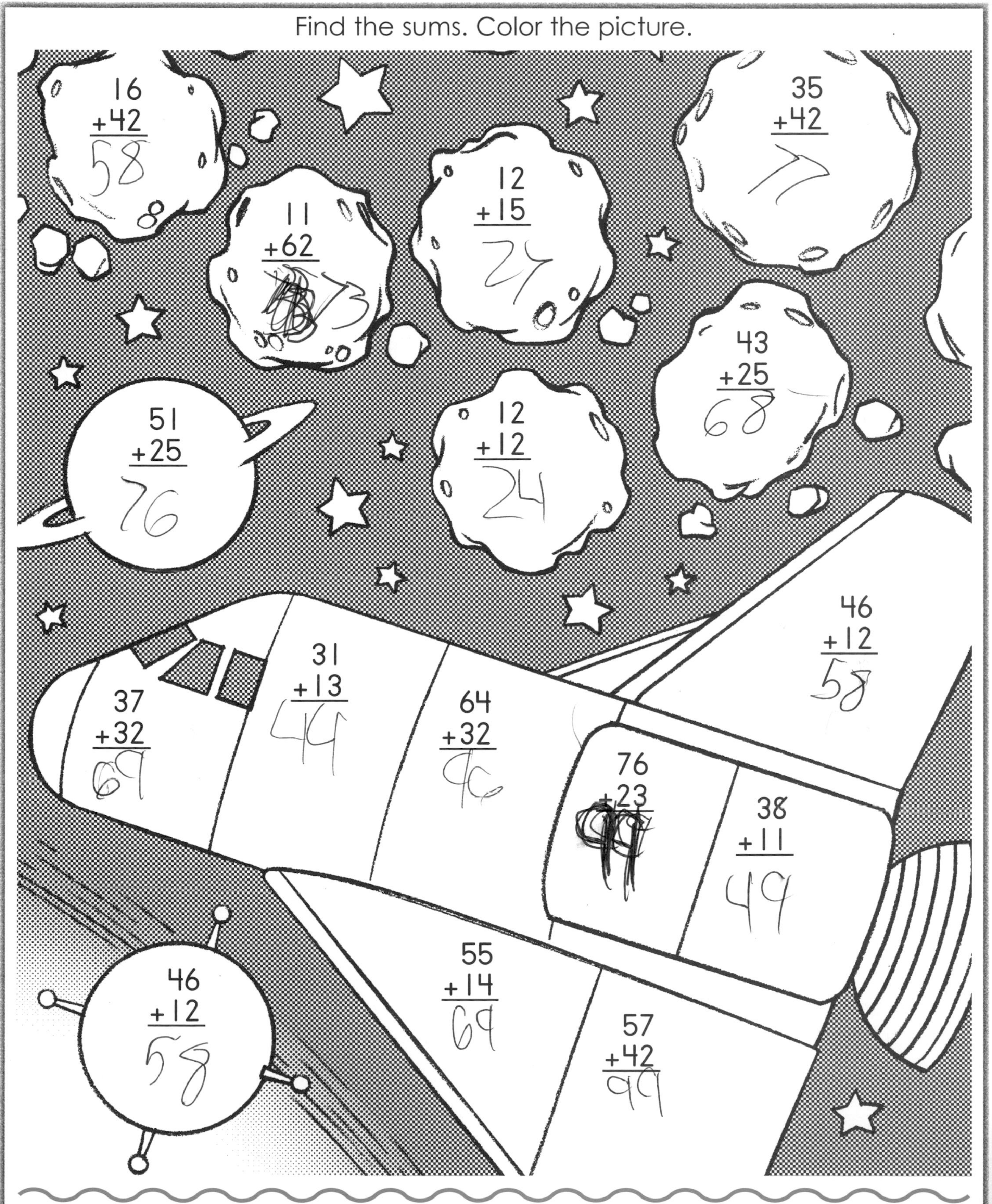

# L Blends: bl, cl, fl, gl, pl, sl

Color the picture with the same **beginning blend** as the first picture.

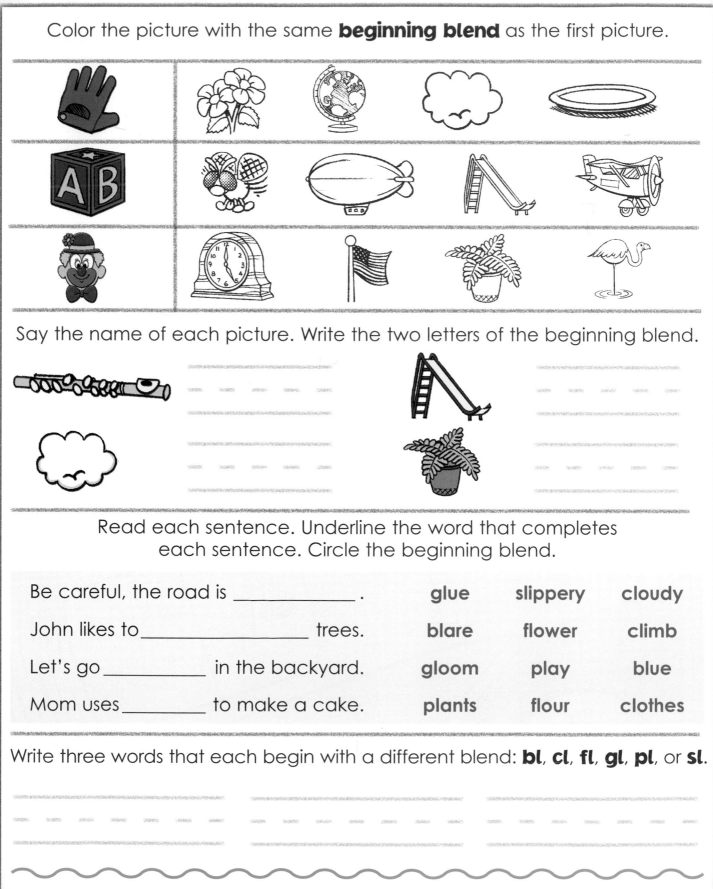

Say the name of each picture. Write the two letters of the beginning blend.

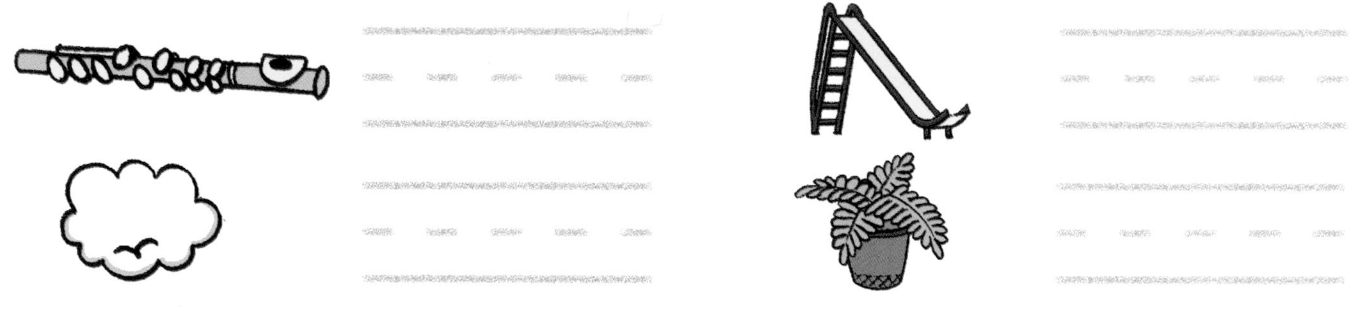

Read each sentence. Underline the word that completes each sentence. Circle the beginning blend.

| | | | |
|---|---|---|---|
| Be careful, the road is ____________ . | **glue** | **slippery** | **cloudy** |
| John likes to________________ trees. | **blare** | **flower** | **climb** |
| Let's go__________ in the backyard. | **gloom** | **play** | **blue** |
| Mom uses________ to make a cake. | **plants** | **flour** | **clothes** |

Write three words that each begin with a different blend: **bl**, **cl**, **fl**, **gl**, **pl**, or **sl**.

# Number Words

Count the dots above each line. Print the correct number word.

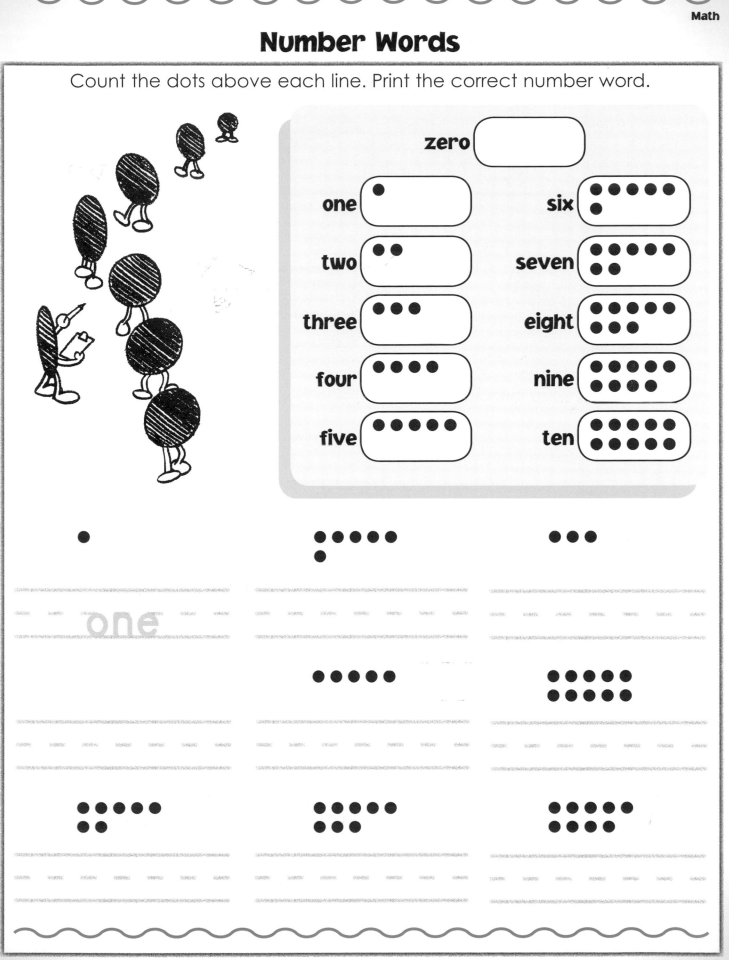

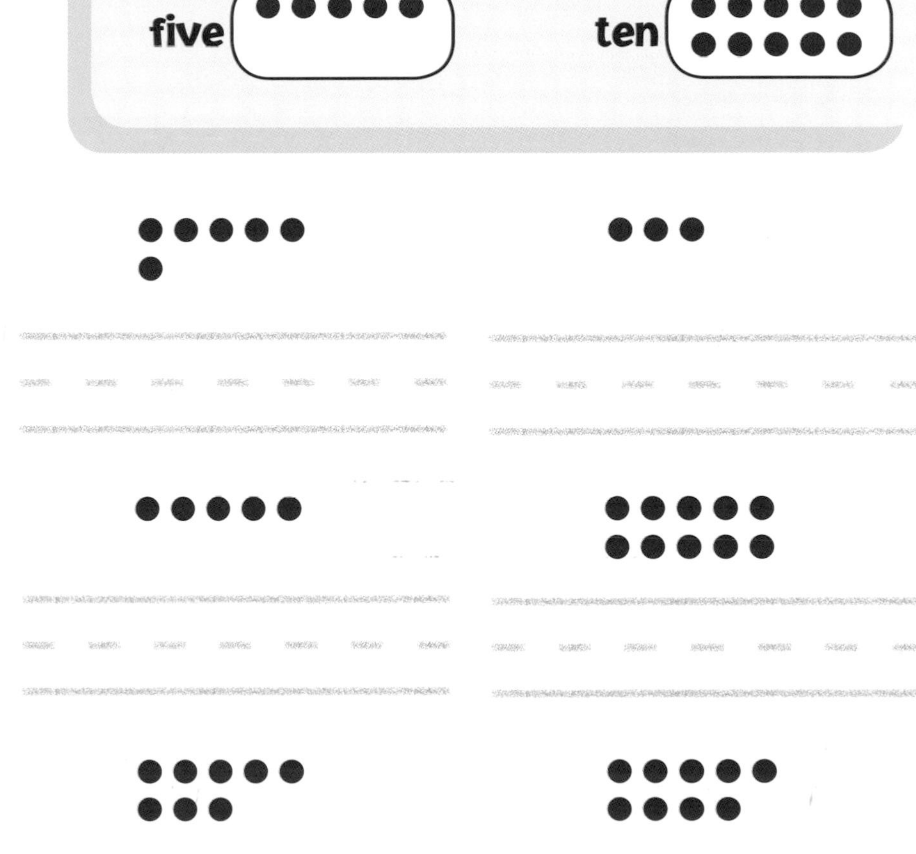

one

# Long ū

Say the words. Listen to the long sound of the vowel **u**.

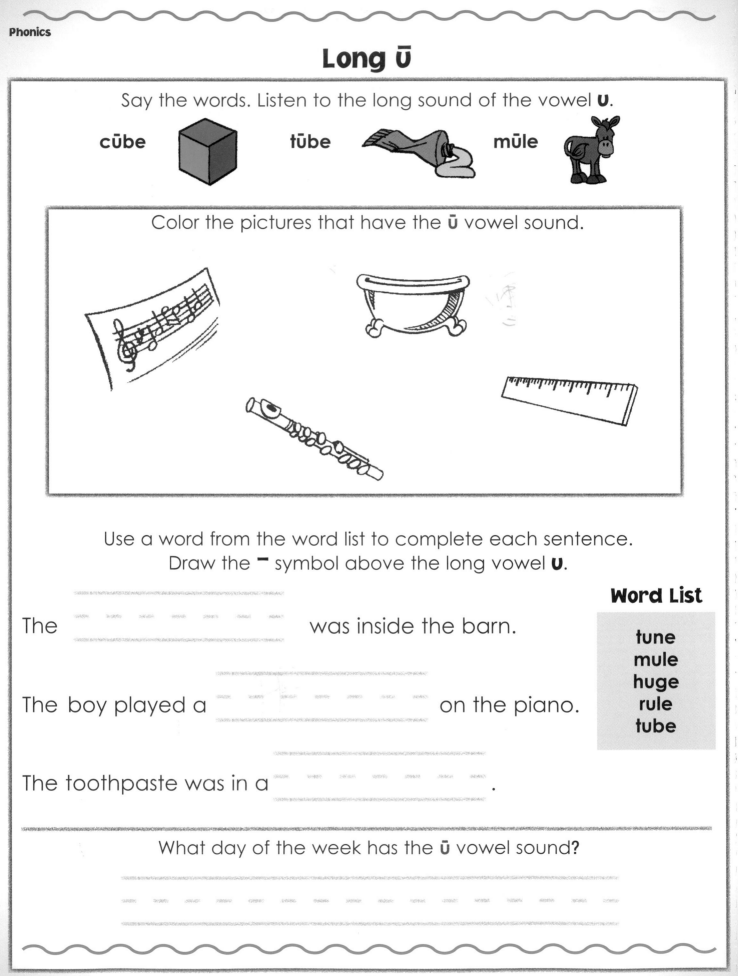

**cūbe**  **tūbe** 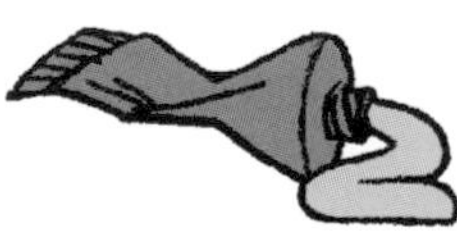 **mūle** 

Color the pictures that have the ū vowel sound.

Use a word from the word list to complete each sentence.
Draw the ¯ symbol above the long vowel **u**.

**Word List**

**tune**
**mule**
**huge**
**rule**
**tube**

The ____________ was inside the barn.

The boy played a ____________ on the piano.

The toothpaste was in a ____________.

What day of the week has the ū vowel sound?

____________

Use the word list to solve the crossword puzzle.

**Word List**

cake
games
ice
gift

**Across**

1. Another word for a present is a ________.
4. We played lots of ________ at the party.

**Down**

2. We had cake and ________ cream.
3. There were many candles on the ________.



Remove pages 93–96. Cut along dashed lines. Staple pages in order.

# My First Crossword Puzzle Book

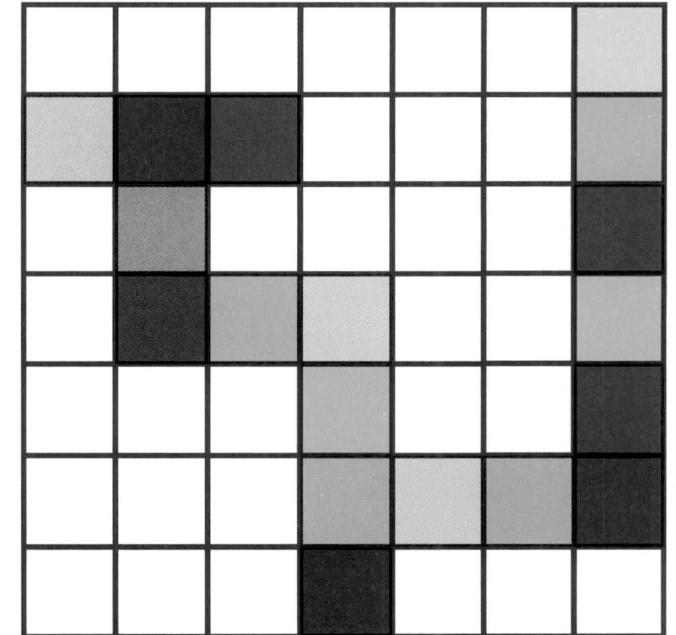

Use the word list to solve the crossword puzzle.

**Word List**

rules
sit
bus
ride

**Across**

3. You must follow the ________ when you ride the bus.

**Down**

1. I ________ the bus to school every day.
2. We wait at the ________ stop.
4. I like to ________ next to my best friend on the bus.



Use the word list to solve the crossword puzzle.

**Word List**

white
milk
straw
ice

**Across**

1. You sip your drink through a ________.
3. Cows give us ________ to drink.
4. Frozen water is called ________.

**Down**

2. The color of vanilla ice cream is ________.

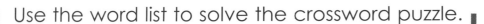

Use the word list to solve the crossword puzzle.

**Word List**

fly
park
tail
year

**Across**

**2.** I fly my kite in the ________.

**3.** Kites, birds, and airplanes can ________.

**Down**

**1.** The ________ is at the end of a kite.

**4.** Spring is the best time of ________ to fly a kite.



Use the word list to solve the crossword puzzle.

**Word List**

save
pigs
dime
bank

**Across**

**2.** Keep your money in a ________.

**4.** A 10¢ coin is a ________.

**Down**

**1.** My bank helps me ________ money.

**3.** Many coin banks look like ________.

Use the word list to solve the crossword puzzle.

**Word List**

eat
pie
tree
fruit

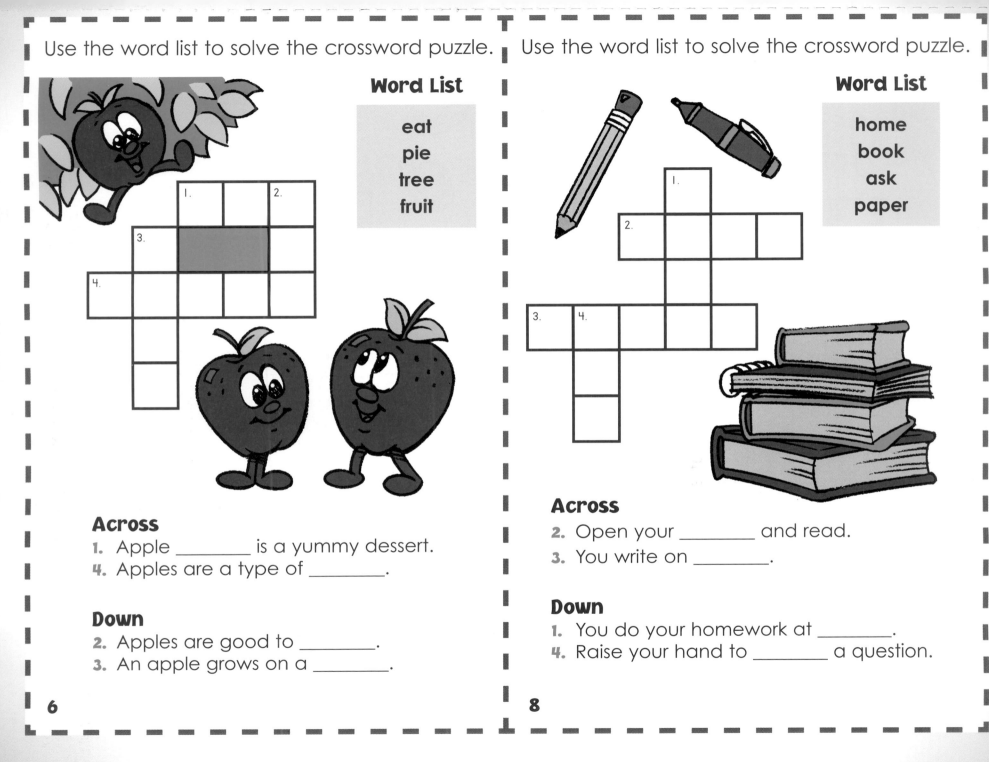

**Across**

1. Apple ________ is a yummy dessert.
4. Apples are a type of ________.

**Down**

2. Apples are good to ________.
3. An apple grows on a ________.

6

Use the word list to solve the crossword puzzle.

**Word List**

home
book
ask
paper

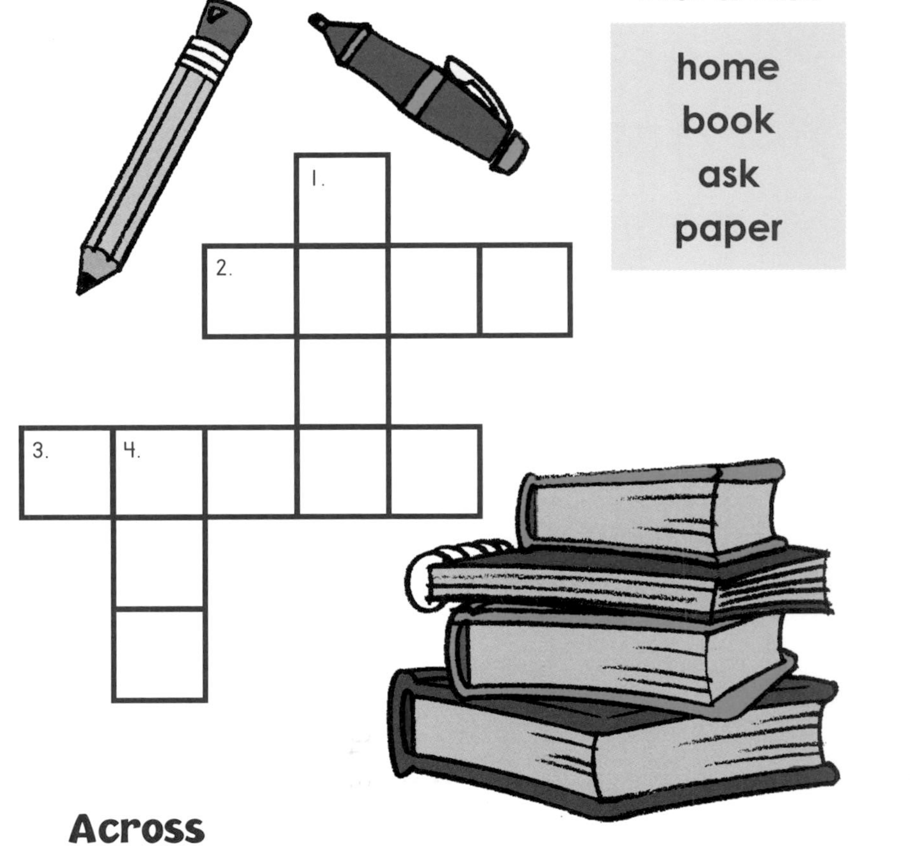

**Across**

2. Open your ________ and read.
3. You write on ________.

**Down**

1. You do your homework at ________.
4. Raise your hand to ________ a question.

8

# R Blends: br, cr, dr, fr, gr, pr, tr

Circle the blend at the beginning of each word. Say the word.

| | | | |
|---|---|---|---|
| 1. proud | 2. brain | 3. dress | 4. crest |
| 5. greet | 6. track | 7. free | 8. drag |
| 9. trampoline | 10. crack | 11. pretend | 12. bring |
| 13. dream | 14. brown | 15. groom | 16. frozen |

Say the name of each picture.
Circle the blend you hear at the beginning of the word.

| | | |
|---|---|---|
| 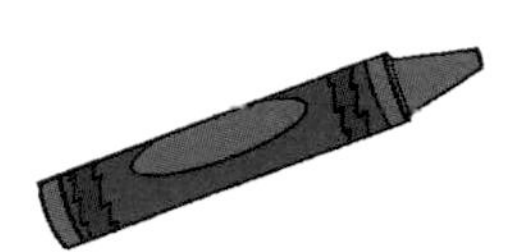 pr fr cr | gr tr cr |  cr fr pr |
|  fr gr tr |  gr dr br |  tr pr cr |

Say the name of each picture. Write the two letters of the beginning blend.

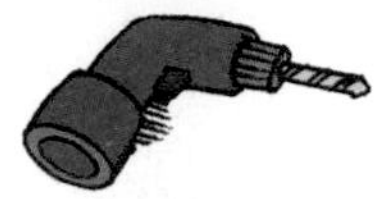

# Calendar Questions

Write the name of the month. Fill in the numbers of the days.

**Month:**

| Sunday | Monday | Tuesday | Wednesday | Thursday | Friday | Saturday |
|---|---|---|---|---|---|---|
| | | | | | | |
| | | | | | | |
| | | | | | | |
| | | | | | | |
| | | | | | | |

**A.** How many days in one week? ______

**B.** How many days in this month? ______

**C.** How many months in a year? ______

**D.** How many seasons in a year? ______

**E.** What is your favorite season? ______

# Greater Than or Less Than?

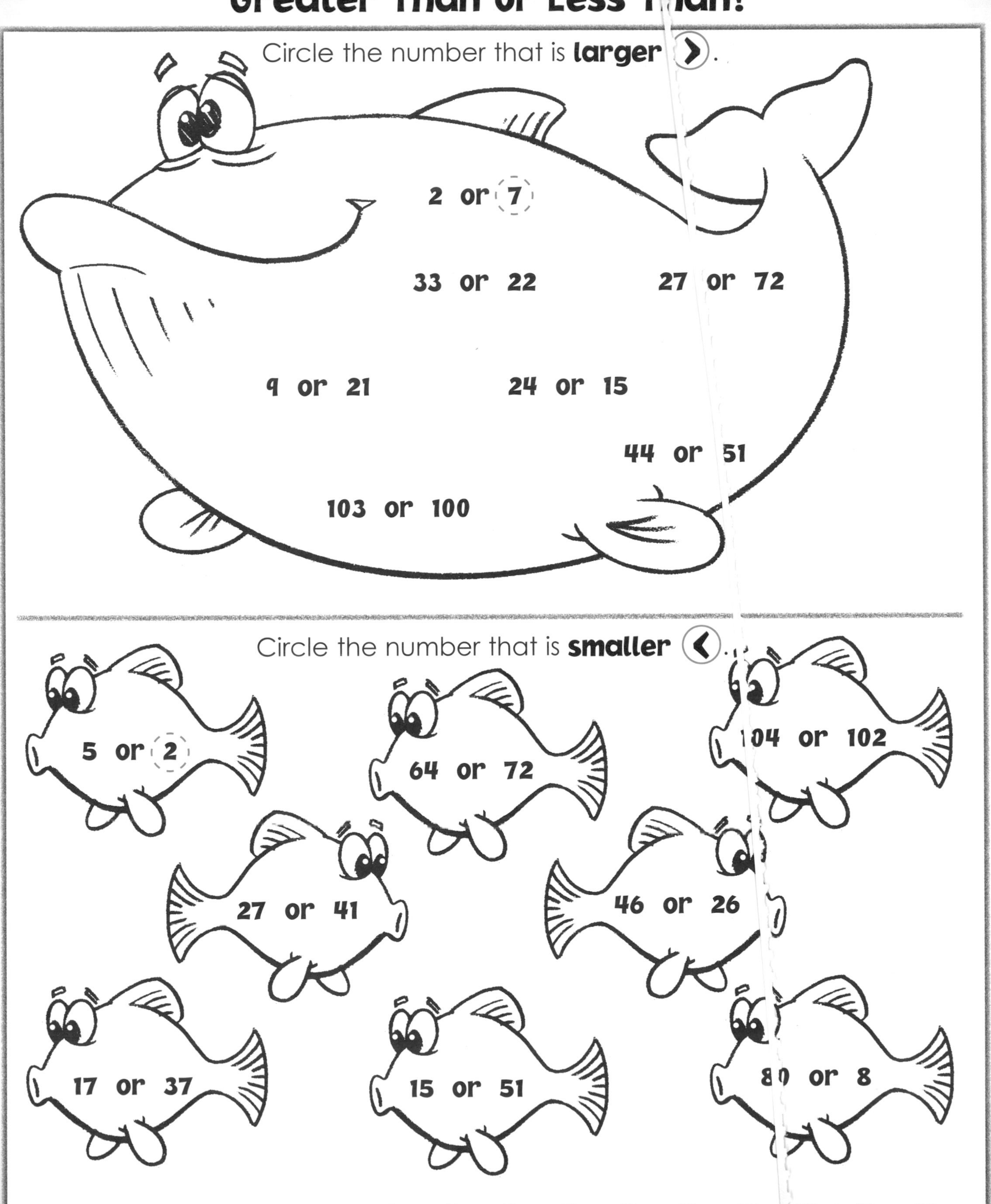

Circle the number that is **larger** (>).
2 or 7
33 or 22
27 or 72
9 or 21
24 or 15
44 or 51
103 or 100
Circle the number that is **smaller** (<).
5 or 2
64 or 72
104 or 102
27 or 41
46 or 26
17 or 37
15 or 51
80 or 8

# Beginning Blends: sk, sm, sn, sp, st, sw, tw

Color the picture with the same **beginning blend** as the first picture.

Circle the blend at the beginning of each word. Say the word.

**1.** ski **2.** twenty **3.** smother **4.** stare **5.** tweezer

**6.** sting **7.** smog **8.** sneeze **9.** spend **10.** swat

Write the word from the word list that completes each sentence. Circle the beginning blend.

I need a ______________ to mail my letter.

Jill and Bill are ______________.

Let's go sledding in the ______________.

Look at the clouds in the ______________!

**Word List**

**sky**
**twins**
**stamp**
**snow**

# Beginning Digraphs: ch, sh, th

Circle the beginning digraph **ch**, **sh**, or **th** in each word. Say the word.

| | | | | |
|---|---|---|---|---|
| 1. chew | 2. thank | 3. three | 4. shock | 5. shut |
| 6. thumb | 7. choose | 8. shape | 9. chime | 10. thing |

Look at the picture in each box. Draw a line from the picture to its name. Circle the beginning digraph.

| | | |
|---|---|---|
|  shirt<br>shine<br>ship |  check<br>child<br>chin |  thunder<br>thin<br>thread |
|  cheer<br>chick<br>cheap |  thimble<br>thumb<br>think |  show<br>shoe<br>shop |

Read the words in the word list. Write each word below its beginning digraph.

**Word List**

| | | |
|---|---|---|
| chip | shy | thumb |
| thin | chin | ship |

| ch | sh | th |
|---|---|---|
| | | |
| | | |

# Calendar Investigation

Trace the numeral 1. Complete the **calendar** by filling in the missing numerals 2–30. Answer the questions below.

## June

| Sunday | Monday | Tuesday | Wednesday | Thursday | Friday | Saturday |
|---|---|---|---|---|---|---|
| | | | 1 | | | |
| | | | | | | |
| | | | | | | |
| | | | | | | |
| | | | | | | |

**A.** On what day of the week does June end? ______________________

**B.** How many Tuesdays are there in June? ______________________

**C.** How many Saturdays are there in June? ______________________

**D.** Are there more Thursdays or Sundays? ______________________

# Beginning Digraph Review: ch, sh, th

Read the words. Write the beginning digraph for each word.

| | | |
|---|---|---|
| **cheek** ______ | **chop** ______ | **shovel** ______ |
| **think** ______ | **sheep** ______ | **thumb** ______ |

Say the name of each picture. Circle the correct beginning digraph.

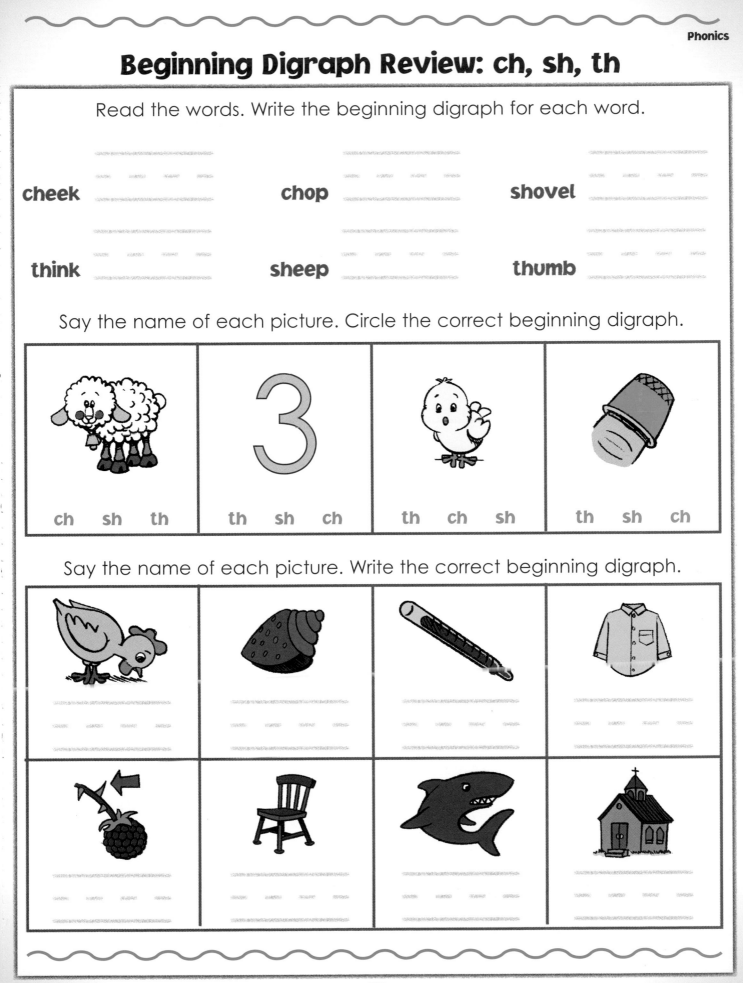

Say the name of each picture. Write the correct beginning digraph.

# Greater/Less

In each box, circle the number that is **greater**.

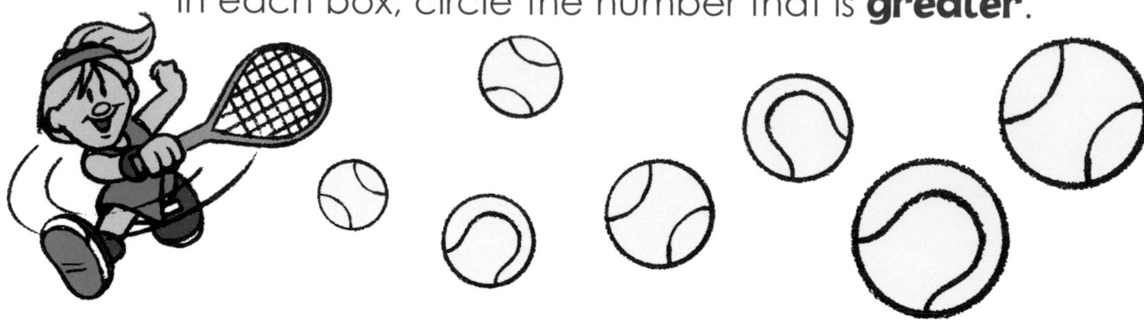

| | | | |
|---|---|---|---|
| 26 30 | 41 29 | 50 20 | 99 100 |
| 11 19 | 67 57 | 84 48 | 72 27 |
| 43 34 | 10 60 | 50 75 | 38 28 |

In each box, circle the number that is **less**.

| | | | |
|---|---|---|---|
| 0 10 | 70 50 | 15 30 | 50 25 |
| 48 24 | 16 32 | 36 72 | 40 80 |
| 29 58 | 19 38 | 42 21 | 100 50 |

Remove pages 117–122. Cut along dashed lines. Staple pages in order.

# The Biggest and Best Book about Me!

**By** ____________________



Draw a picture of yourself in the frame below.
Color the picture.

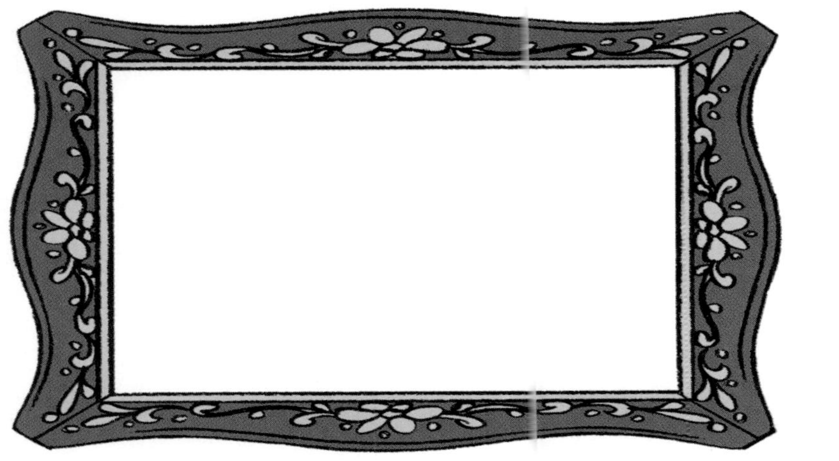

Describe yourself. Use the words in the word list to complete the sentences.

**Word List**

| | | |
|---|---|---|
| green | blue | gray |
| brown | black | red |
| hazel | long | curly |
| straight | short | blonde |

I have ____________________ eyes.

I have ____________________ hair.

My hair is ____________________.

Complete the sentences below. Use the answers to write a story about yourself on a separate sheet of paper.

My name is ______________________.

My favorite color is. ______________________.

Write some words that tell about you. Use the words in the word list.

**Word List**

| | |
|---|---|
| special | helpful |
| shy | friendly |
| nice | busy |
| fun | kind |
| quiet | happy |

Draw some of your favorite things next to the toy box. Color your pictures. Complete the sentences below.

My favorite game is ______________________.

My favorite book is ______________________.

My favorite toy is ______________________.

Tell about your family.

Fill in the correct numbers.

I have . . . ☐ brother(s). ☐ sister(s).

☐ uncle(s). ☐ aunt(s).

☐ cousin(s).

Check one.

I am . . . ☐ the oldest.

☐ in the middle.

☐ the only child.

☐ the youngest.



Read the sentences. Draw a picture in each box.

| | |
|---|---|
| This makes me **happy**. | This makes me **angry**. |
| This **surprises** me. | This makes me **laugh**. |
| This makes me **scared**. | This makes me **proud**. |

Tell about the pictures you drew on page 5.

I feel **happy** when

I feel **angry** when

I feel **surprised** when

I **laugh** when

I feel **scared** when

I feel **proud** when

Today I feel

6

Families have different rules to keep everyone safe and happy. Write some of the rules in your family.

**A safety rule in my family is**

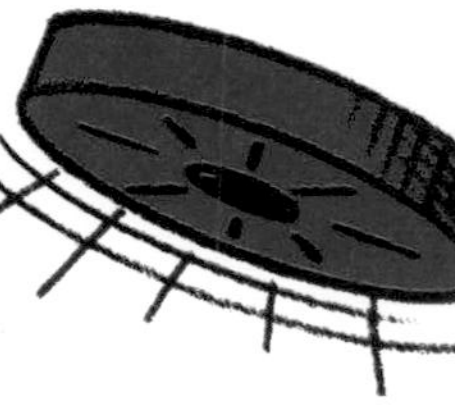

**A cleanup rule in my family is**

8

Complete each sentence.
Draw a picture for each sentence.

My family has fun when

My family works together when



Families have different rules
to keep everyone safe and happy.
Write some of the rules in your family.

**A bedtime rule in my family is**

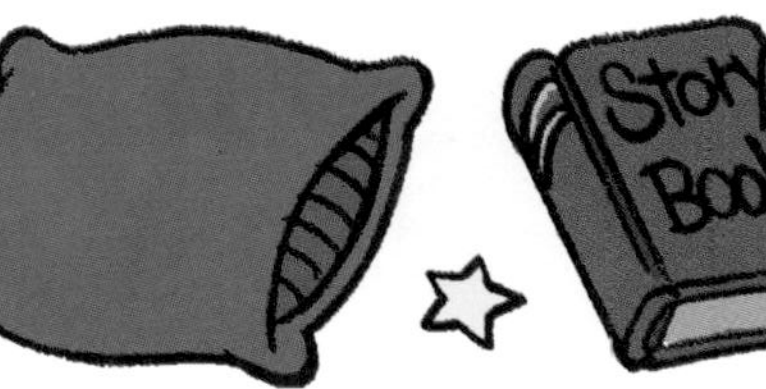

**A rule just for me is**

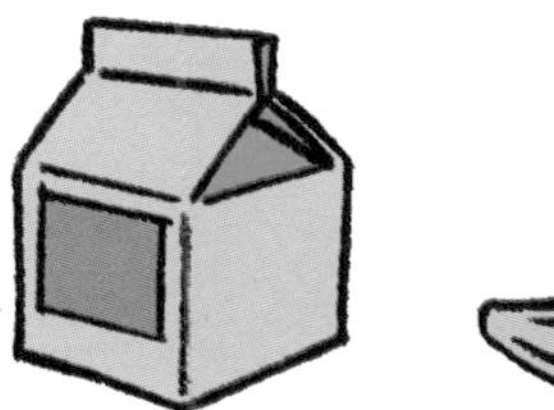

Families work together and help each other. Write about how you help the people in your family.

Every day I ______________________.

A special job I have is ______________________.

My favorite job is ______________________.

I enjoy helping my ______________________.

10

12

This is a picture of me and my family at home.

# Ending Digraphs: -ch, -sh, -th

Read the words. Circle the ending digraph **ch**, **sh**, or **th** in each word.

1. coach
2. dish
3. mouth
4. moth
5. bush
6. couch
7. trash
8. much

Say the name of each picture. Fill in the circle next to the ending digraph.

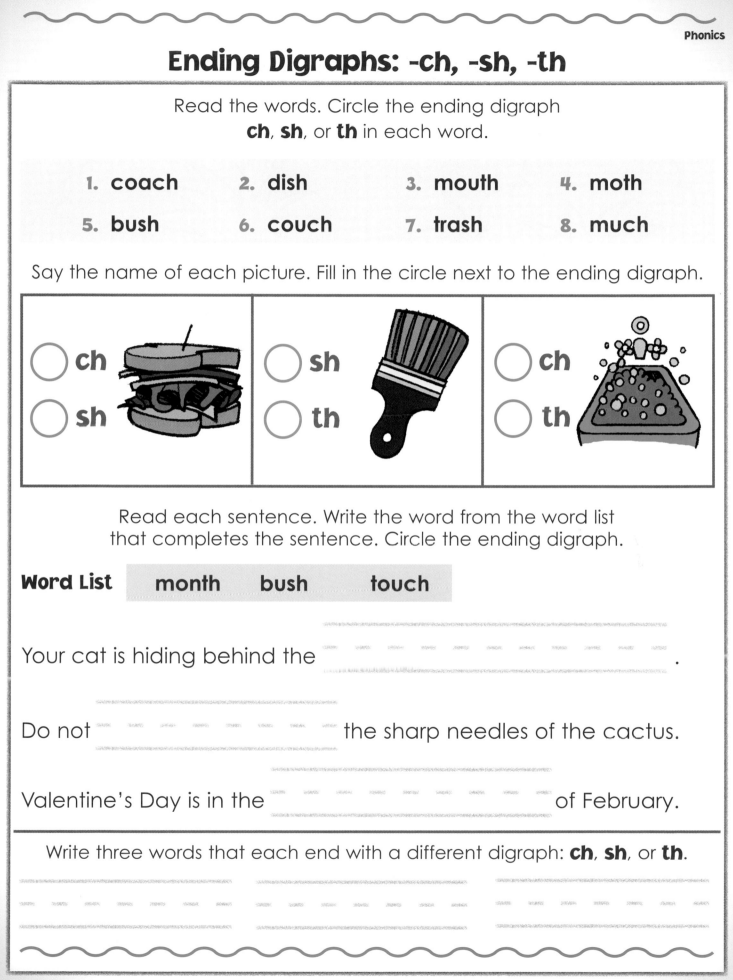

Read each sentence. Write the word from the word list that completes the sentence. Circle the ending digraph.

**Word List** month bush touch

Your cat is hiding behind the ______________.

Do not ______________ the sharp needles of the cactus.

Valentine's Day is in the ______________ of February.

Write three words that each end with a different digraph: **ch**, **sh**, or **th**.

______________ ______________ ______________

# Following Directions

Follow the directions to complete the picture.

1. Draw two little ducks behind the others.
2. Color the biggest duck yellow.
3. Draw a plant by the pond.
4. Make a nest near the pond.
5. Color each duck a different color.
6. Circle the smallest duck.
7. Color the water blue.
8. Color the plants green.

# Match the Opposites

Draw lines to match the pictures that are **opposites**.

left

day

night

right

dry

sad

happy

wet

# Subtraction Review

Fill in the missing numbers.

| | | |
|---|---|---|
| 16 − ☐ = 8 | 15 − ☐ = 9 | 17 − ☐ = 8 |
| 14 − ☐ = 8 | 10 − ☐ = 6 | 8 − ☐ = 0 |
| 6 − ☐ = 4 | 9 − ☐ = 9 | 12 − ☐ = 7 |

# Ending Digraph -ng

Write the **ng** digraph at the end of each set of letters. Say the words.

cla ______ wro ______ bri ______

si ______ lu ______ stro ______

Look at the picture in each box. Write the **ng** word that names the picture and circle the ending digraph.

| swing wrong | sing thing | bring wing |
|---|---|---|
| ______ | ______ | ______ |

Read each sentence and the words below it. Write the **ng** word that completes each sentence.

I like to ______ in music class.

bring sing ding

I'm sorry, but that answer is ______.

wrong song long

# How Much Does It Cost?

Write the price next to each object.
Add to find out how much two toys cost.

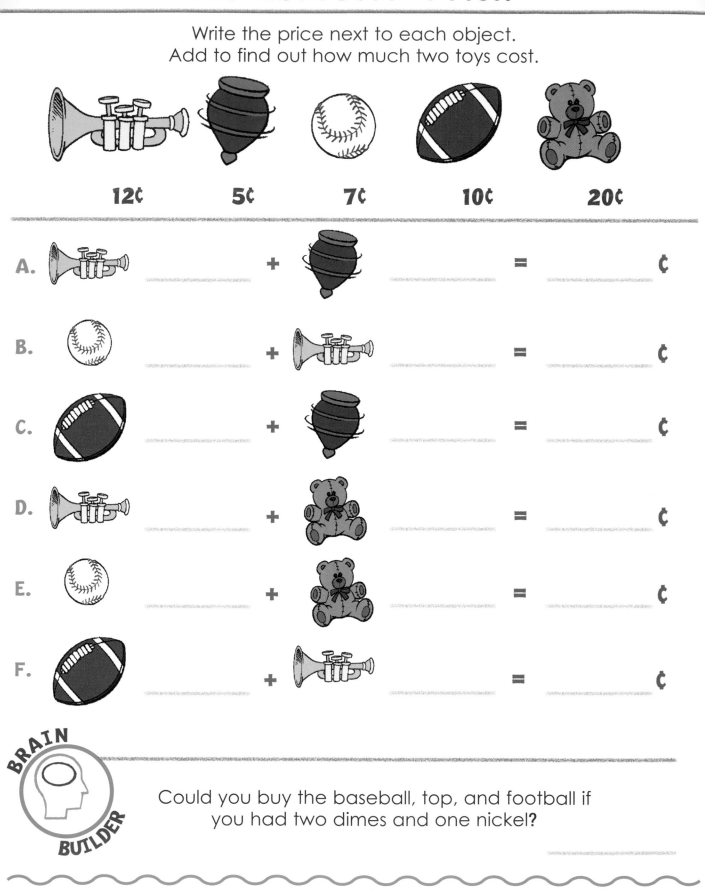

**12¢** **5¢** **7¢** **10¢** **20¢**

A. ______ +  ______ = ______ ¢

B.  ______ + 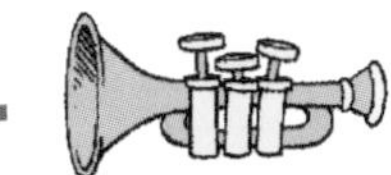 ______ = ______ ¢

C.  ______ +  ______ = ______ ¢

D. 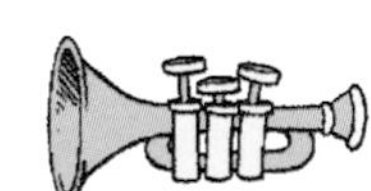 ______ +  ______ = ______ ¢

E.  ______ +  ______ = ______ ¢

F.  ______ + 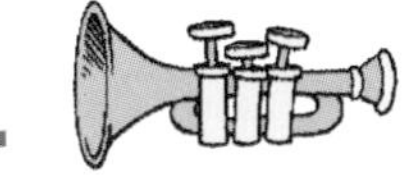 ______ = ______ ¢

Could you buy the baseball, top, and football if you had two dimes and one nickel?

______

# Homonym Crossword Puzzle

**Homonyms** are words that sound alike.
Complete the puzzle using the homonyms from the word list.

**Word List**

| blue | hear | four | our |
|---|---|---|---|
| plane | pail | eight | right |

**Across**

1. for
4. ate
6. plain
7. blew

**Down**

2. hour
3. write
5. here
6. pale

# Three-Addend Addition

Sometimes in addition, **three** numbers are added together. To find the sum, add the first two addends together, then add the third addend.

**4 + 3 + 5 = 12**

**Think . . . 4 + 3 = [ 7 ], then [ 7 ] + 5 = 12**

$$\begin{array}{r} 7 \\ 4 \\ +\ 2 \\ \hline \square \end{array} \qquad \begin{array}{r} 6 \\ 5 \\ +\ 3 \\ \hline \square \end{array} \qquad \begin{array}{r} 4 \\ 4 \\ +\ 3 \\ \hline \square \end{array} \qquad \begin{array}{r} 4 \\ 3 \\ +\ 6 \\ \hline \square \end{array}$$

$$\begin{array}{r} 4 \\ 2 \\ +\ 5 \\ \hline \square \end{array} \qquad \begin{array}{r} 4 \\ 6 \\ +\ 2 \\ \hline \square \end{array} \qquad \begin{array}{r} 7 \\ 2 \\ +\ 4 \\ \hline \square \end{array} \qquad \begin{array}{r} 8 \\ 8 \\ +\ 1 \\ \hline \square \end{array}$$

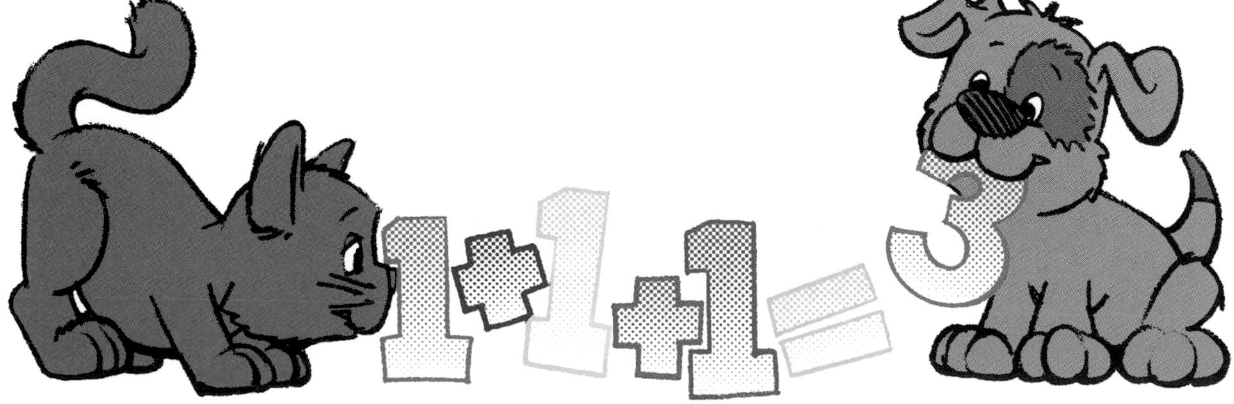

# Ending Digraph Review: -ch, -sh, -th, -ng

Say each word. Fill in the circle if the word ends with the digraph **ch**, **sh**, **th**, or **ng**.

○ junk ○ king ○ sandwich ○ hat

○ booth ○ glee ○ most ○ wish

Say the name of each picture. Circle the correct ending digraph.

| | | | |
|---|---|---|---|
| sh th | ng sh | ch th | sh ng |
| ch th | ng th | ng sh | th sh |

Read each word and circle the ending digraph. Draw a line from each word to its picture.

tooth

sandwich

king

brush

# Story Time

Read the story. Draw how you think the story will end.

Frog liked to sit on a lily pad in the pond. He loved to catch bugs, too. When he ate too many bugs, the lily pad sank into the water.

Write a sentence to tell about your picture.

# Fractions (½)

Color ½ of each shape.

Brian had six mini pizzas for his party. He cut each pizza in half. How many halves did he have in all?

# R-Controlled Vowel ar

Say the name of each picture. Listen to the **ar** sound.

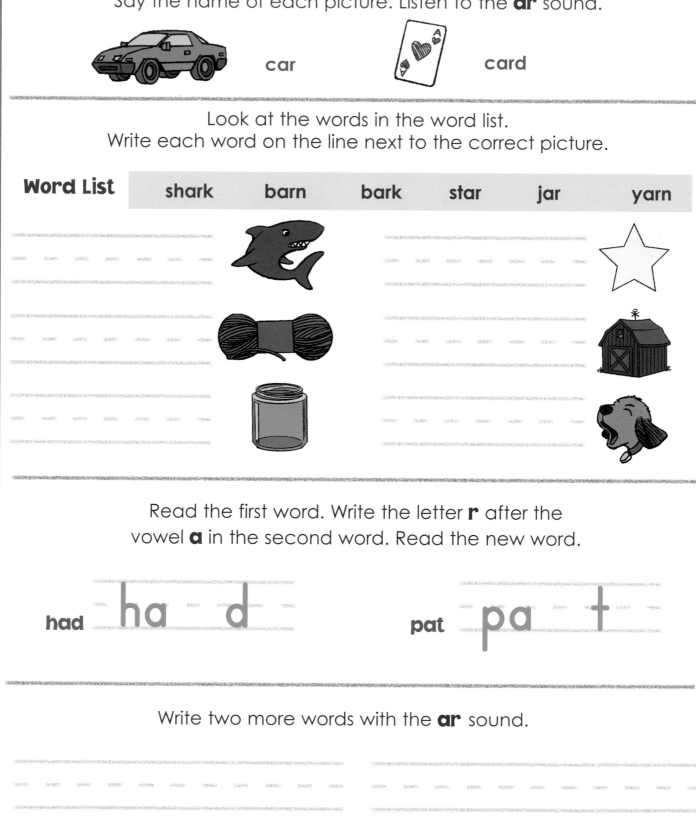

car

card

Look at the words in the word list.
Write each word on the line next to the correct picture.

| **Word List** | shark | barn | bark | star | jar | yarn |
|---|---|---|---|---|---|---|

Read the first word. Write the letter **r** after the vowel **a** in the second word. Read the new word.

pat pa t

Write two more words with the **ar** sound.

# Hit the Target Math

Subtract. Cut out and glue the arrow with the correct answer to each target.

62
- 10

41
- 20

62
- 21

39
- 17

75
- 52

81
- 20

90
- 80

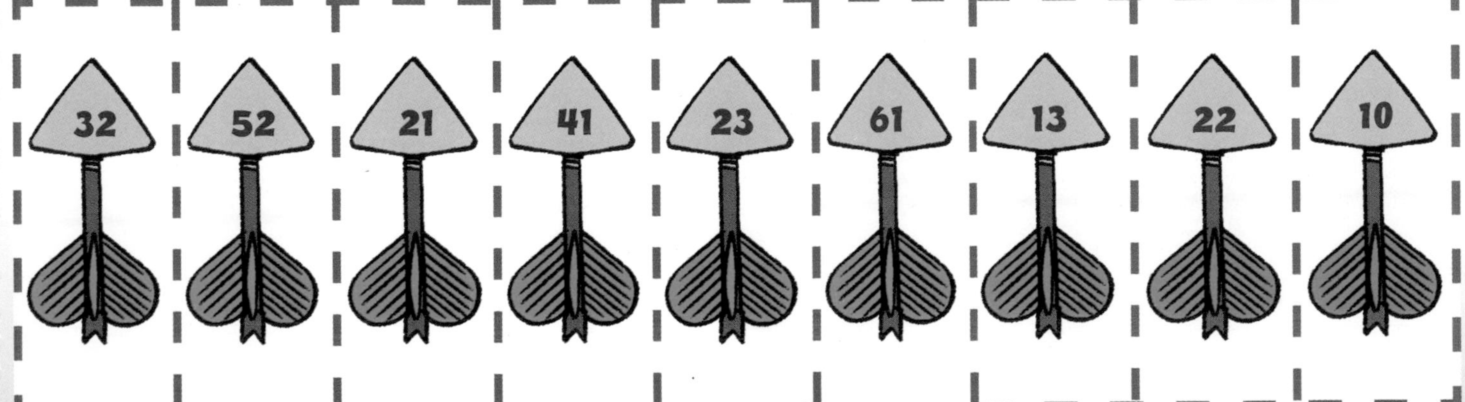

Remove pages 139—142. Cut along dashed lines. Staple pages in order.
See directions on page 142.

# My Own Story

**Written and Illustrated by**

1

3

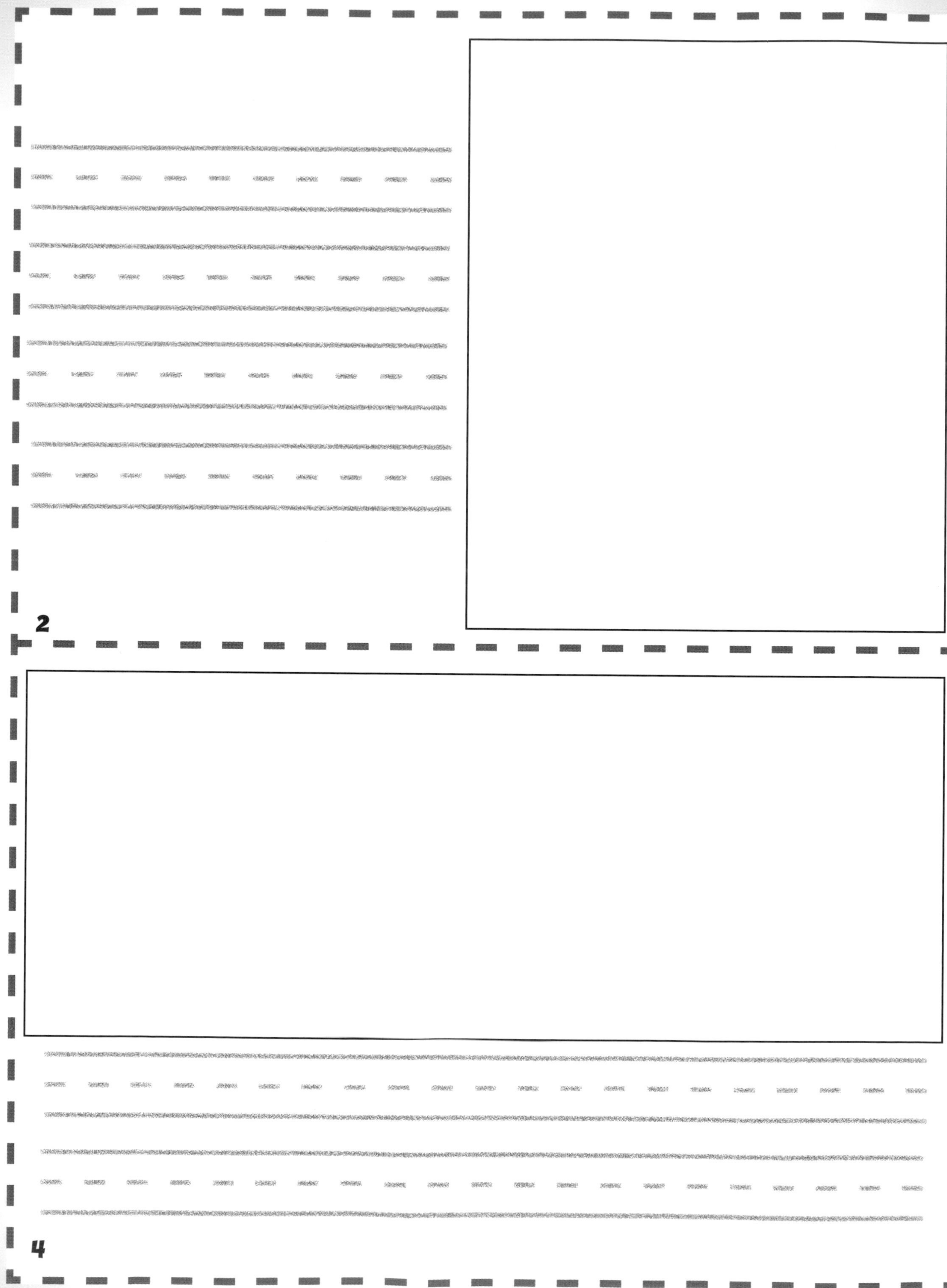
2
4

5

7

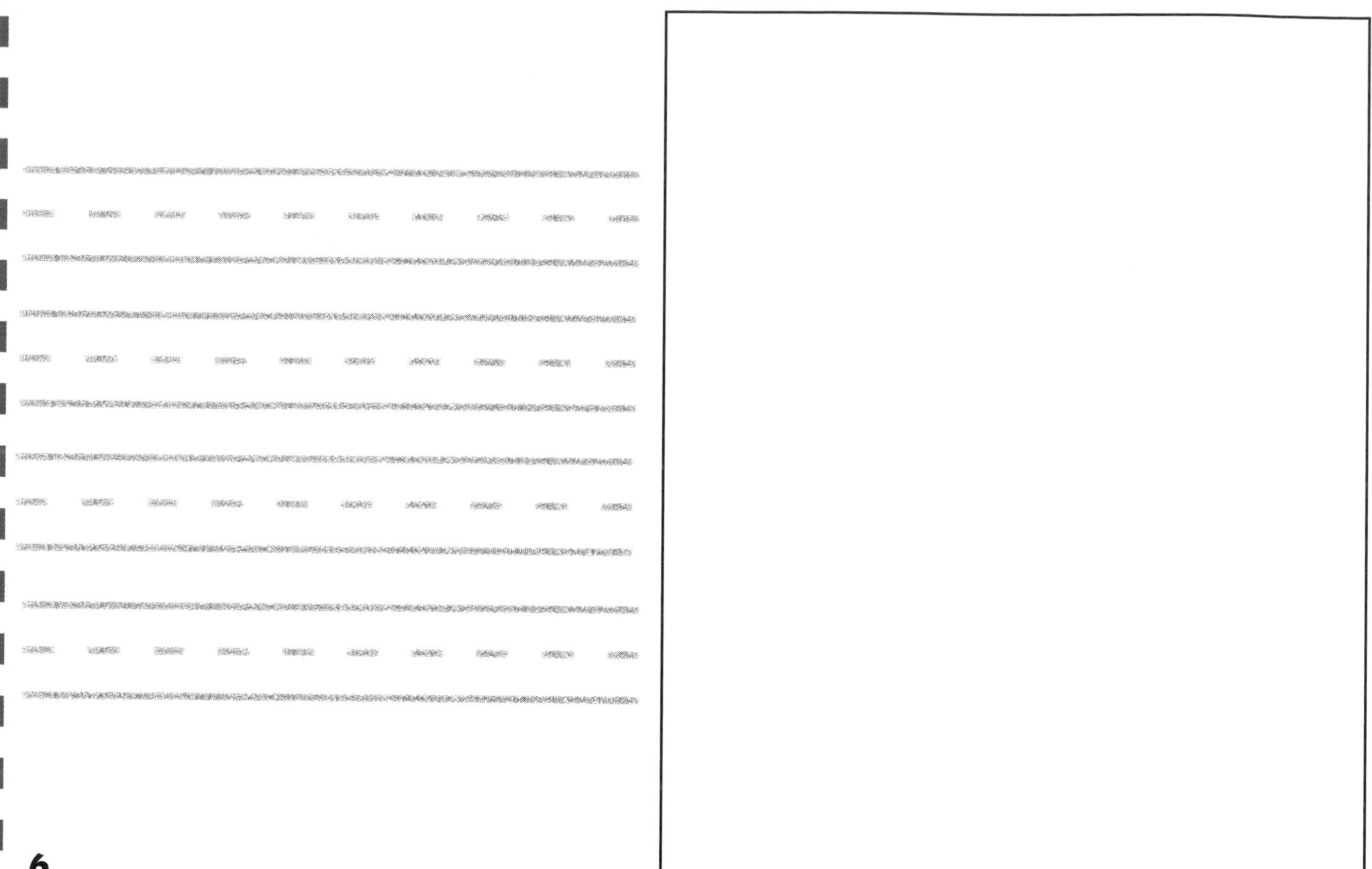

6

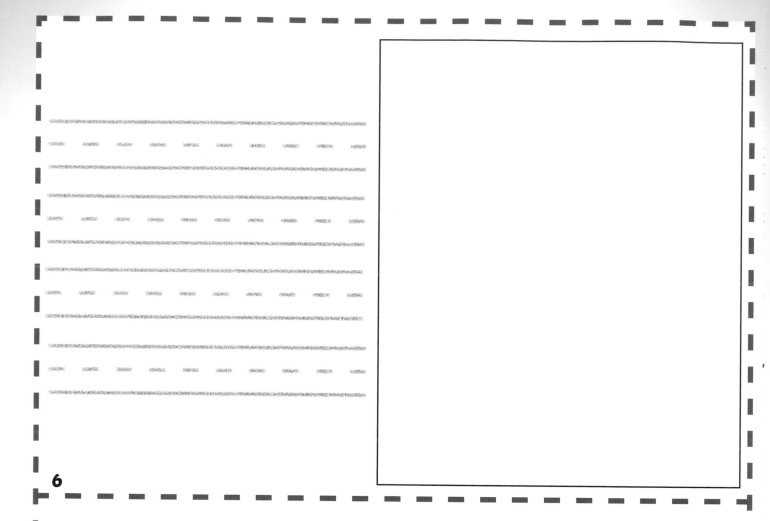

You have permission to photocopy pages 139–142. Let your child practice writing and illustrating a story. For many children entering second grade, six pages will be too many pages to write. Let your child decide how long and how many pages the story will be when it is finished.

Do not "over-correct." To become a good writer, one has to practice. Children who are overly criticized will not want to practice, and writing could become an unpleasant experience.

Encourage your child to be creative and imaginative. Help your child discover how much fun it is to learn to write!

# Coloring Fractions

Color the objects divided into **halves** red.
Color the objects divided into **thirds** blue.
Color the objects divided into **fourths** green.

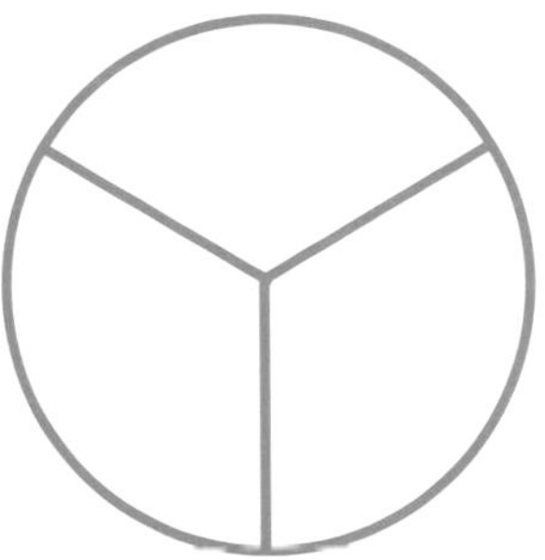

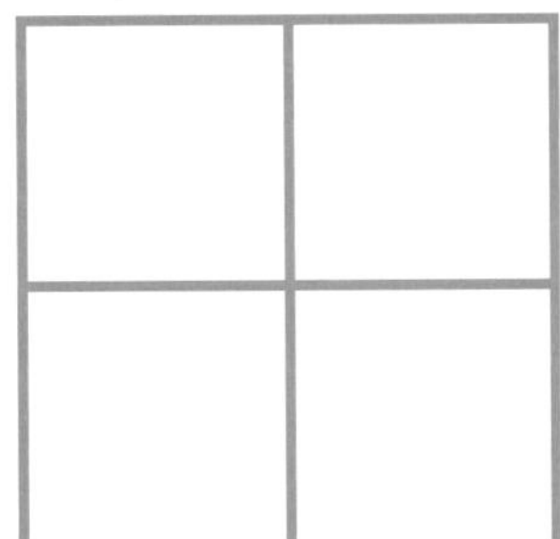

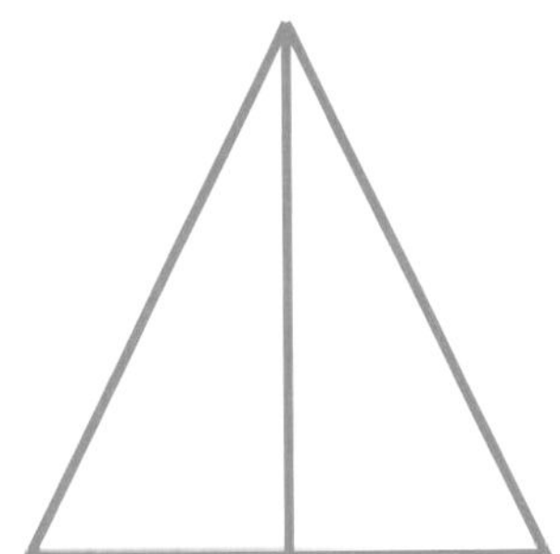

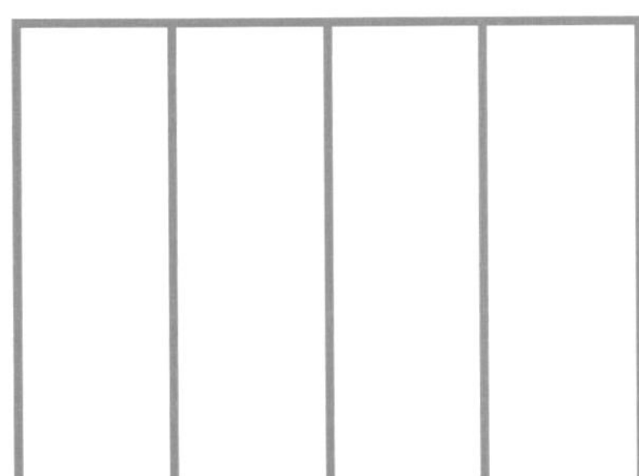

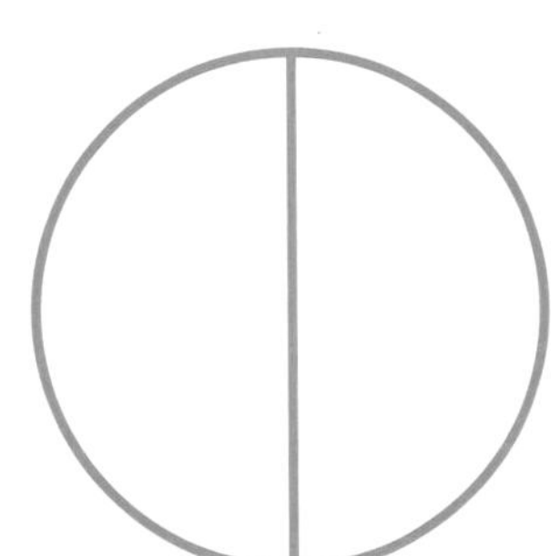

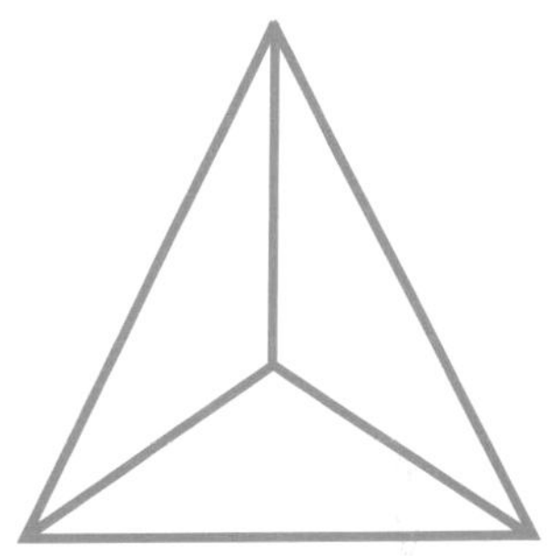

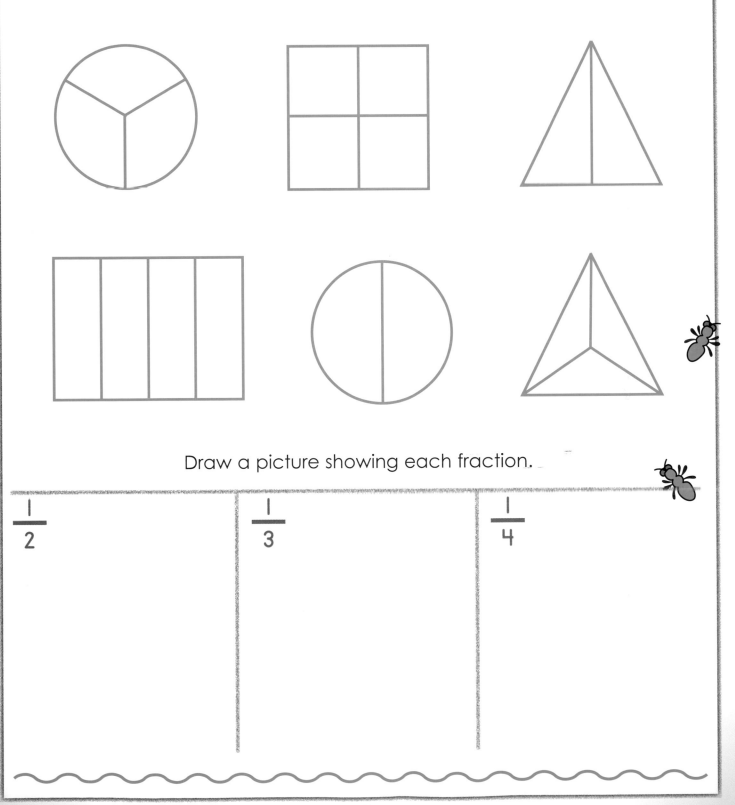

Draw a picture showing each fraction.

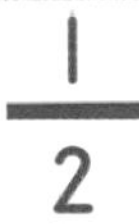


$\frac{1}{3}$

# Beginning and Ending Digraphs

Read the words. Circle the beginning or ending digraph in each word.

| | | | |
|---|---|---|---|
| 1. cheese | 2. south | 3. ring | 4. crush |
| 5. think | 6. shingle | 7. touch | 8. shampoo |
| 9. thorn | 10. such | 11. wish | 12. sing |

Read each sentence. Write the words that begin or end with **ch**, **sh**, **th**, or **ng** digraphs. Circle each digraph.

**The mouse had a piece of cheese in its mouth.**

**A very short king must wear a small robe.**

Say the name of each picture.
Write the correct beginning or ending digraph.

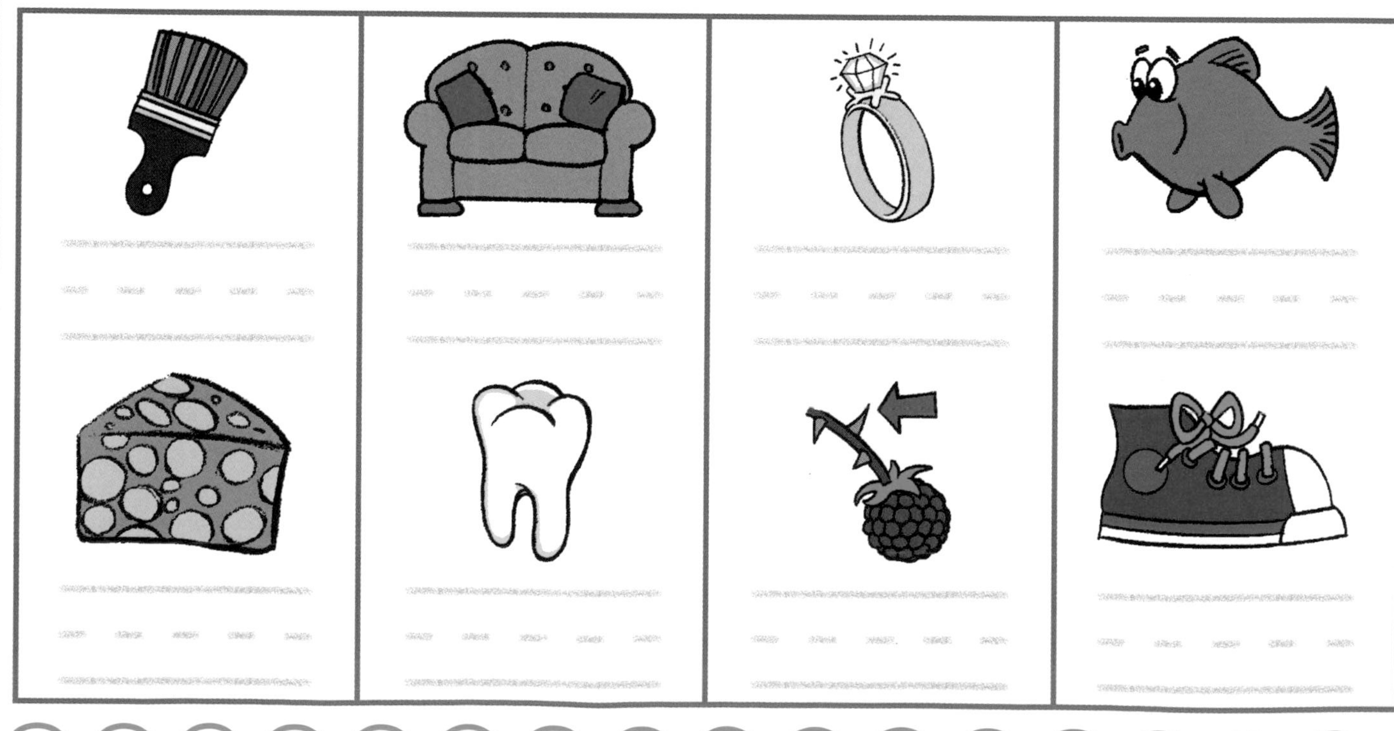

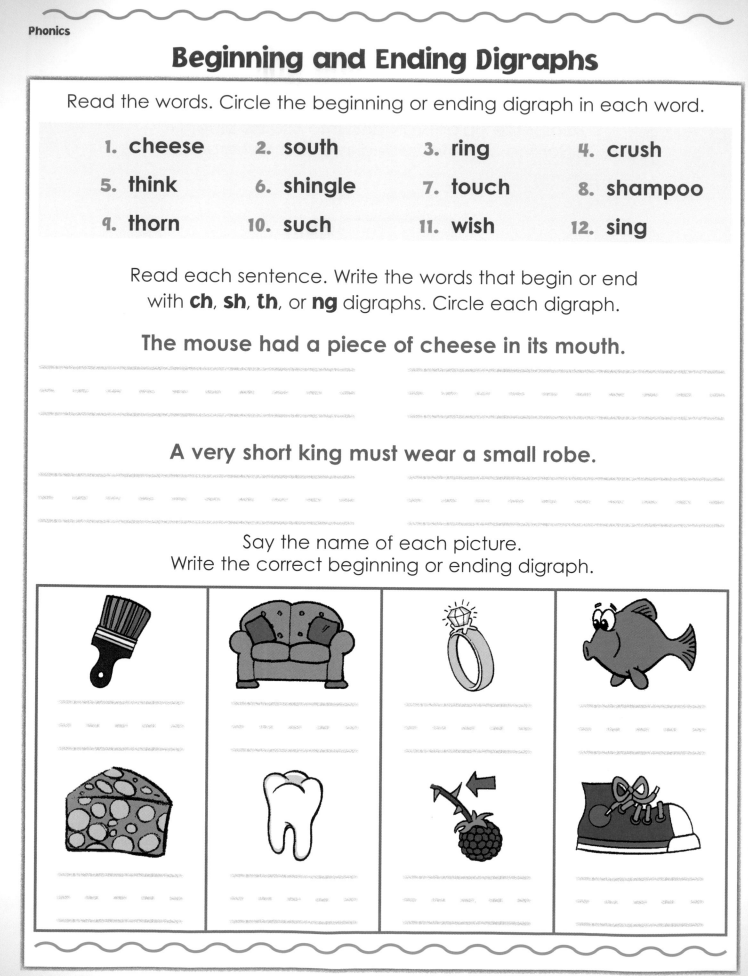

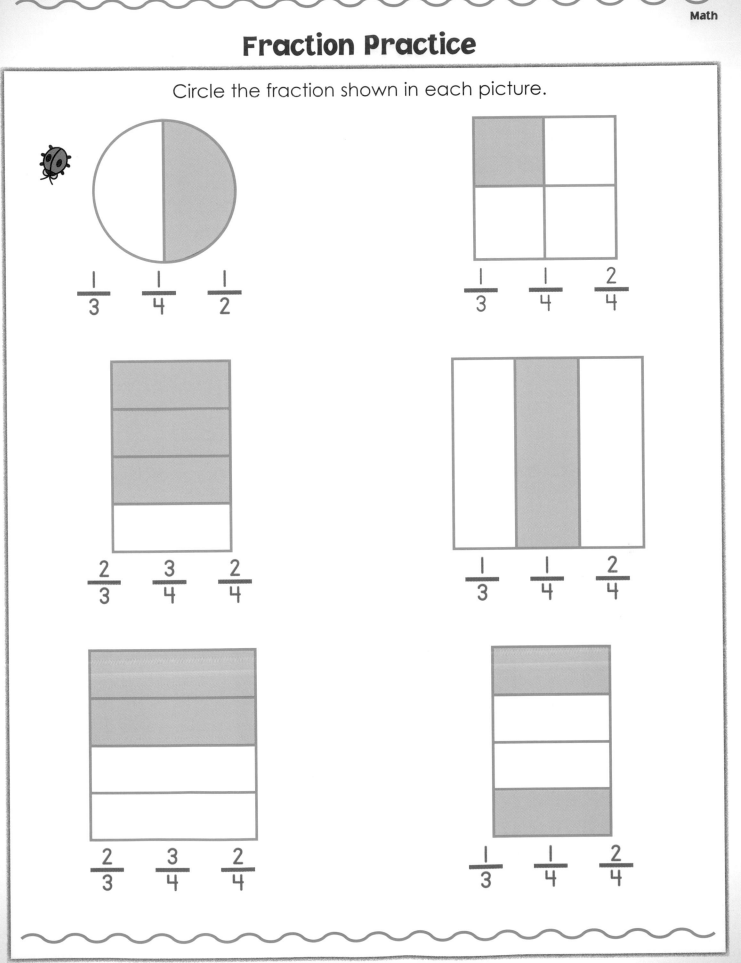

# Fraction Practice

Circle the fraction shown in each picture.

$\frac{1}{3}$ $\frac{1}{4}$ $\frac{1}{2}$

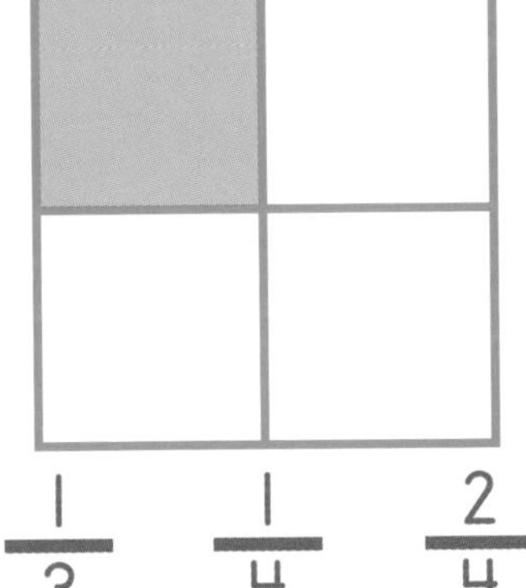

$\frac{1}{3}$ $\frac{1}{4}$ $\frac{2}{4}$

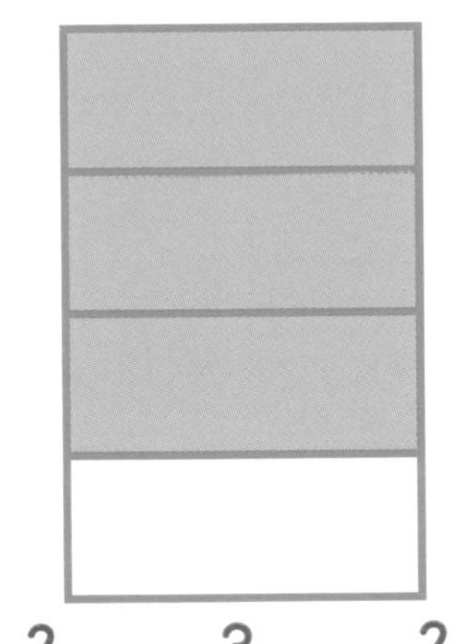

$\frac{2}{3}$ $\frac{3}{4}$ $\frac{2}{4}$

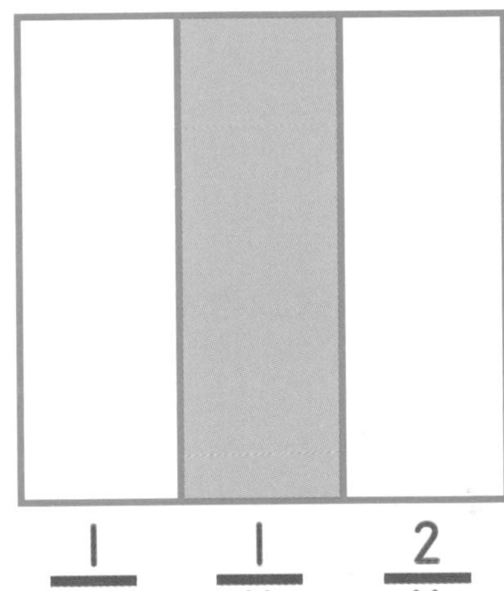

$\frac{1}{3}$ $\frac{1}{4}$ $\frac{2}{4}$

$\frac{2}{3}$ $\frac{3}{4}$ $\frac{2}{4}$

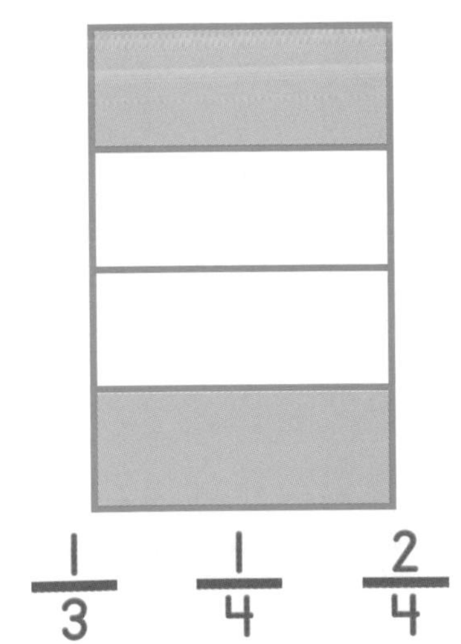

$\frac{1}{3}$ $\frac{1}{4}$ $\frac{2}{4}$

# R-Controlled Vowel er

Say the name of each picture. Listen to the **er** sound.

hammer 

fern 

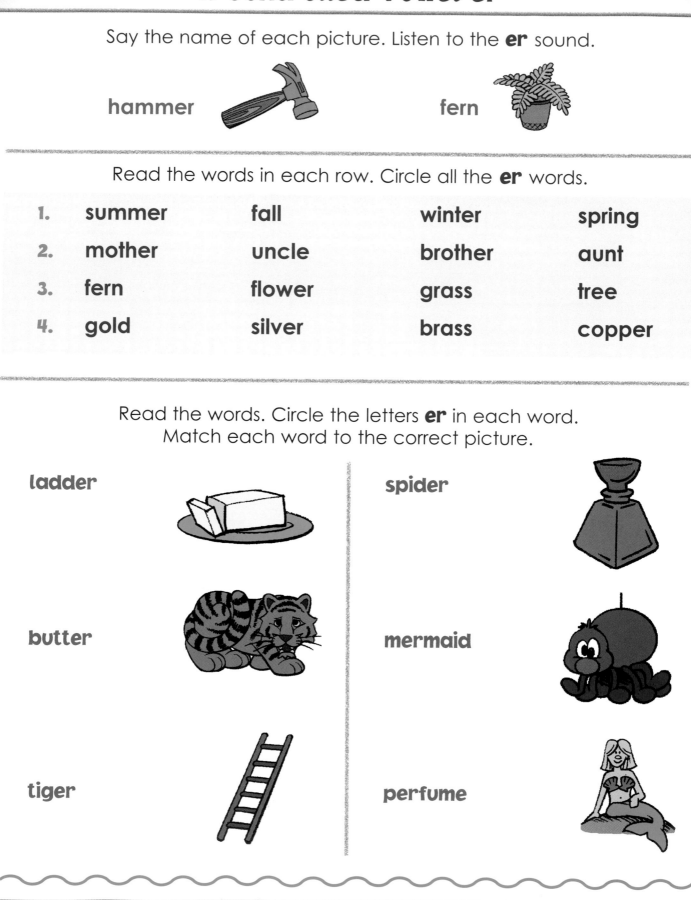

Read the words in each row. Circle all the **er** words.

| | | | | |
|---|---|---|---|---|
| 1. | summer | fall | winter | spring |
| 2. | mother | uncle | brother | aunt |
| 3. | fern | flower | grass | tree |
| 4. | gold | silver | brass | copper |

Read the words. Circle the letters **er** in each word.
Match each word to the correct picture.

ladder

butter

tiger

spider

mermaid

perfume

# R-Controlled Vowel ir

Say the name of each picture. Listen to the **ir** sound.

girl 

bird 

Say the name of each picture. Listen to the **ir** sound.
Write the letters **ir** to complete each word.

 sk ___ t

 d ___ t

th ___ ty

 sh ___ t

f ___ st

 st ___

Read the words in the word list. Choose the best words to complete the sentences. Circle the letters **ir** in each word.

The ____________ is in town.

Watch me ____________ this baton.

**Word List**

**circle**
**circus**
**third**
**twirl**

# Reading a Chart

Each first grade student at Washington Elementary has chosen a flavor of ice cream to have at a school party. Look at the chart and answer the questions below.

| Flavor of Ice Cream | Number of Students |
|---|---|
| chocolate | 47 |
| vanilla | 32 |
| strawberry | 17 |
| banana | 10 |
| butter pecan | 5 |

**A.** Which flavor of ice cream was chosen by the most students? ______________________

**B.** Which flavor of ice cream was chosen by the fewest students? ______________________

**C.** How many more students chose chocolate than vanilla? ______________________

**D.** How many more students chose strawberry than butter pecan? ______________________

**E.** How many more students chose chocolate than banana? ______________________

**F.** What is the total number of students that chose strawberry or vanilla? ______________________

**G.** What is the total number of students that chose vanilla or butter pecan? ______________________

**H.** What is the total number of students that chose chocolate or vanilla? ______________________

# R-Controlled Vowel or

Say the name of each picture. Listen to the **or** sound.

horn 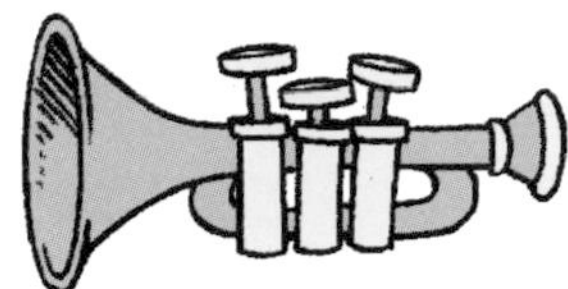

fork 

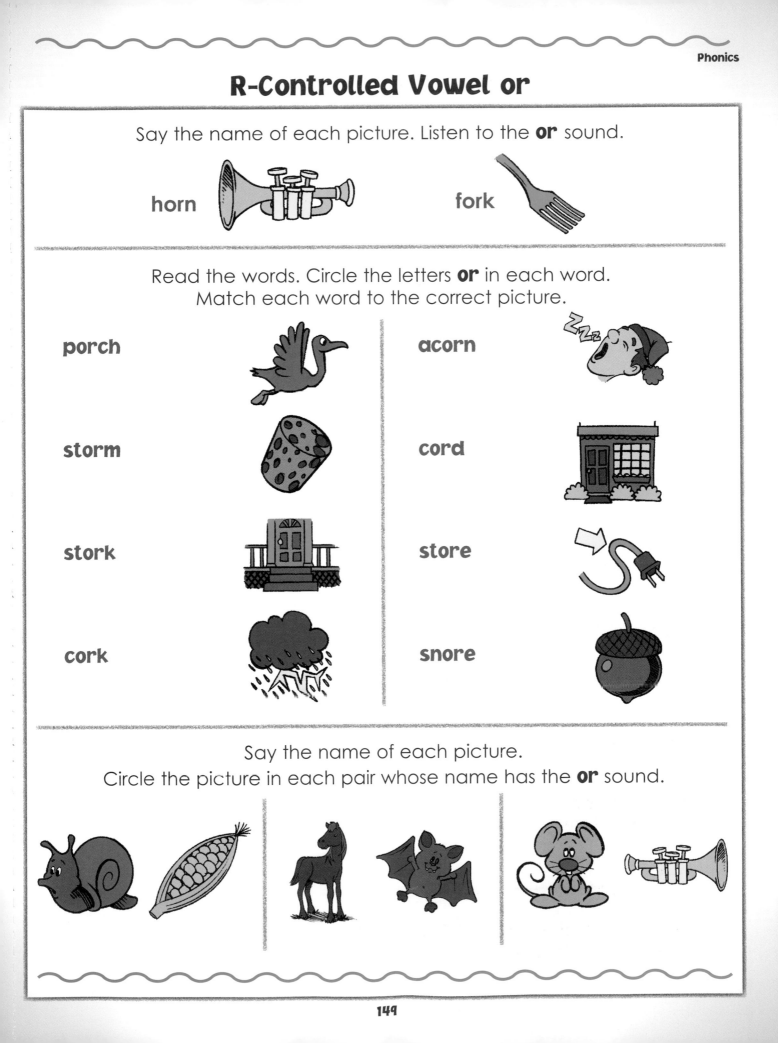

Read the words. Circle the letters **or** in each word.
Match each word to the correct picture.

**porch** 

**storm** 

**stork** 

**cork** 

**acorn** 

**cord** 

**store** 

**snore** 

Say the name of each picture.
Circle the picture in each pair whose name has the **or** sound.

 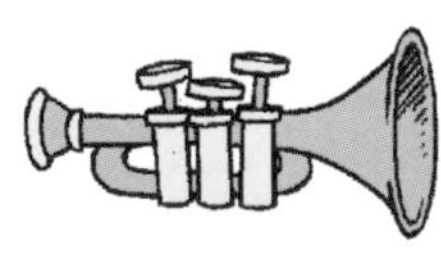

# R-Controlled Vowel ur

Say the name of each picture. Listen to the **ur** sound.

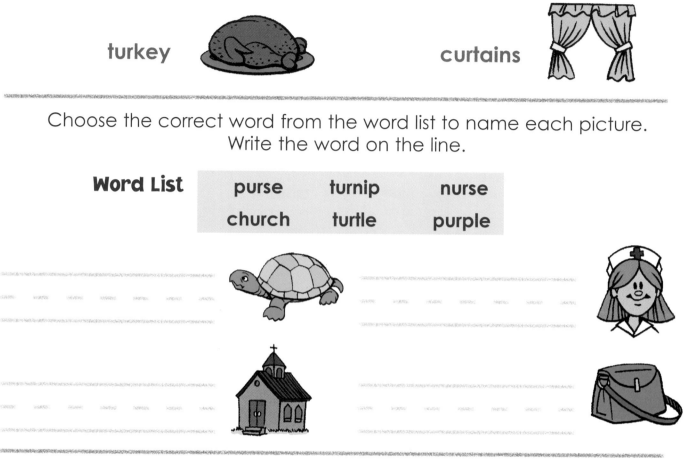

turkey  curtains 

Choose the correct word from the word list to name each picture. Write the word on the line.

**Word List**

| purse | turnip | nurse |
|---|---|---|
| church | turtle | purple |

Read each sentence. Circle the **ur** word in each sentence.

1. We had turkey for dinner.
2. The school nurse treated me.
3. Please return the books to Tim.
4. I hurt my leg when I fell.
5. Will you please turn on the radio?

# Cut-and-Paste Synonyms

**Synonyms** are words that have the same or nearly the same meaning. Cut and paste to match the synonyms.

| happy | ill | couch |
|---|---|---|
| | | |

| angry | skinny | friends |
|---|---|---|
| | | |

sick

mad

thin

pals

glad

sofa

# Money Problems

Solve the word problems.

**A.** Susan had a nickel. She found another nickel. Her mother gave her two dimes for taking out the trash. How much money does she have now?

________________ ¢

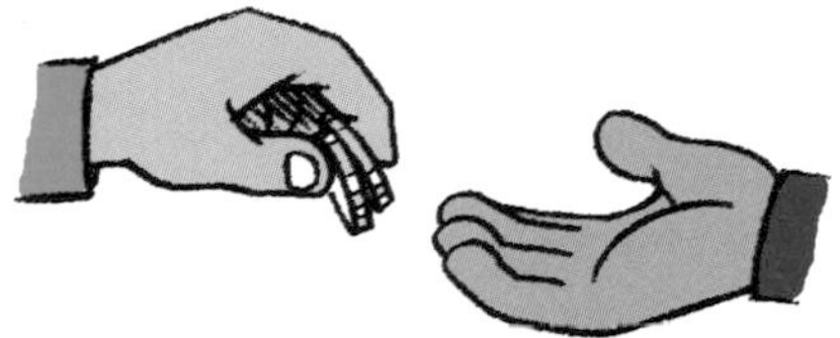

**B.** Tyrone wants to buy ice cream at lunch. Lunch costs 50¢ and ice cream costs 25¢. If Tyrone has $1.00, does he have enough to buy both?

**Yes** **No**

**C.** Maria took 50¢ to the store. She spent 10¢ on candy, 10¢ on popcorn, and 15¢ on a drink. How much money did she spend?

________________ ¢

How much does she have left?

________________ ¢

# Y as a Vowel

When **y** is at the end of a word,
it can make the long sound of the vowel **e** or **i**.

**baby (ē)**  **cry (ī)** 

Read the name of each picture. Listen to the sound of the letter **y**.
Circle the vowel sound made by the letter **y**.

 **sky** ē ī

 **city** ē ī

 **jewelry** ē ī

 **fly** ē ī

Read the words in the word list. Listen to the sound of the letter **y**.
List the words under the correct sound.

**Word List** tiny why silly try

| ē | ī |
| --- | --- |
| | |
| | |

# Cut-and-Paste Antonyms

**Antonyms** are words that have opposite meanings.
Cut and paste to match the antonyms.

in

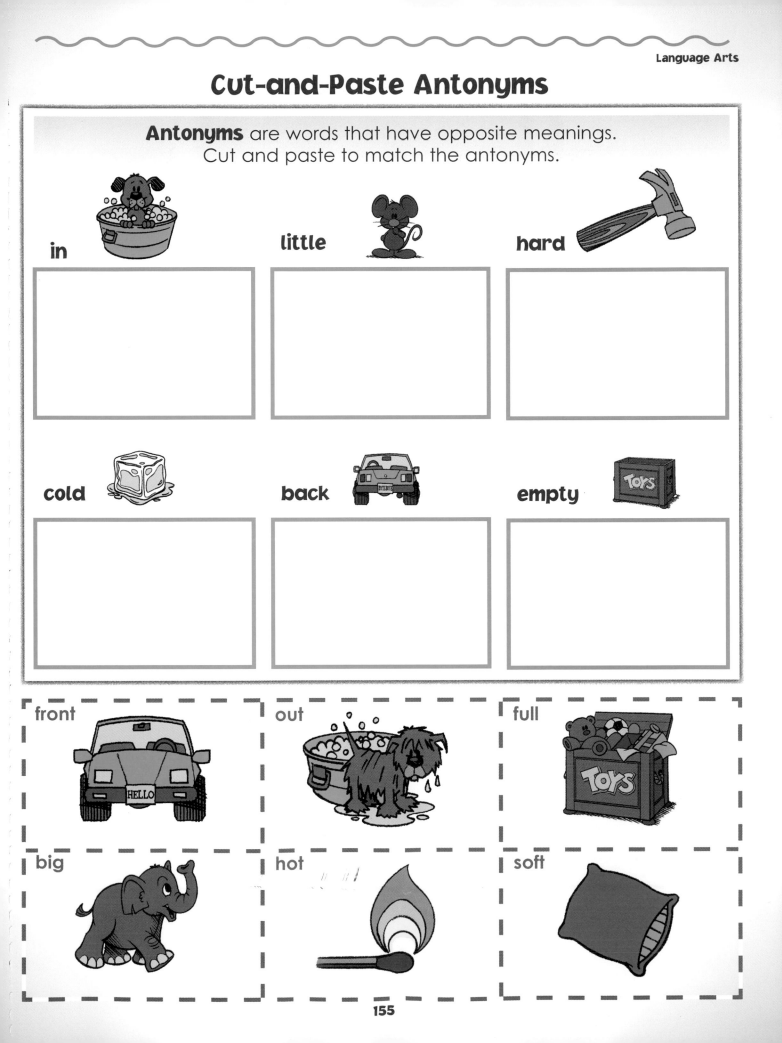

little

hard

cold

back

empty

front

out

full

big

hot

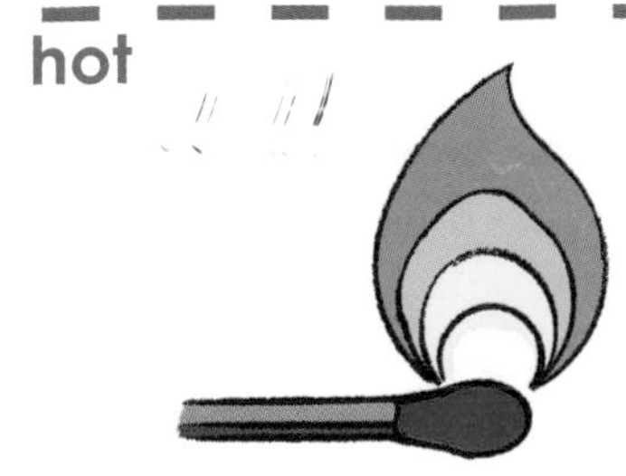

soft

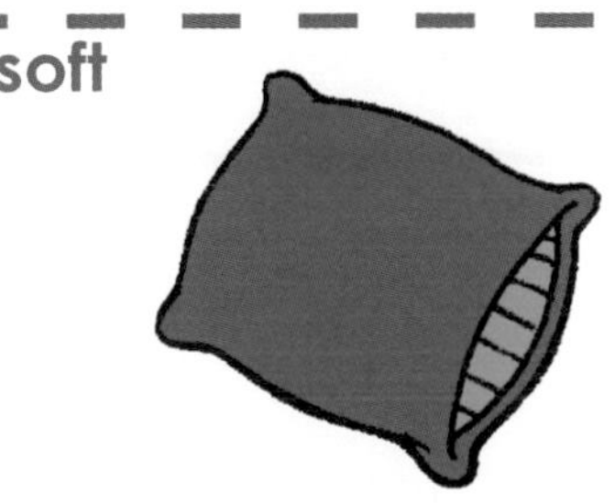

# Reproducible Creative Writing Paper

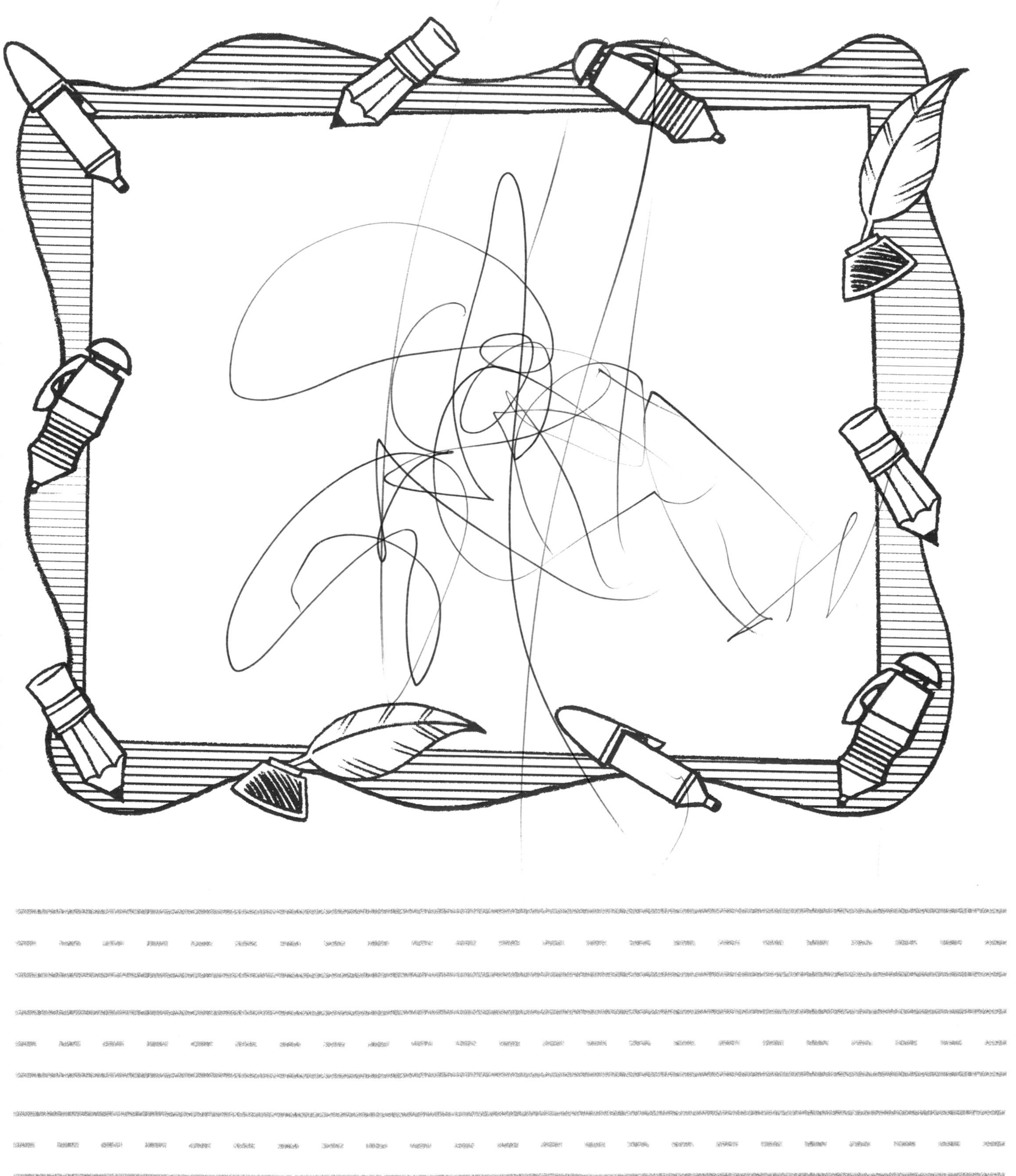

# Reproducible Creative Writing Paper

50¢

# Daily News

MORNING EDITION

# Cut-and-Color Awards

Parent: Have your child decorate and color these awards. Fill in your child's name and the date to mark each accomplishment. The awards can be worn as badges or put into small frames.

I can tell time on the hour and half hour.

Name: ______________ Date: ________

I know my + and − facts to 18.

Name: ______________ Date: ________

I know all my short vowels.

Name: ______________ Date: ________

I know all my long vowels.

Name: ______________ Date: ________

I can measure with a ruler using inches or centimeters.

Name: ______________ Date: ________

I can add and subtract two-digit numbers.

Name: ______________ Date: ________

I can count money using:

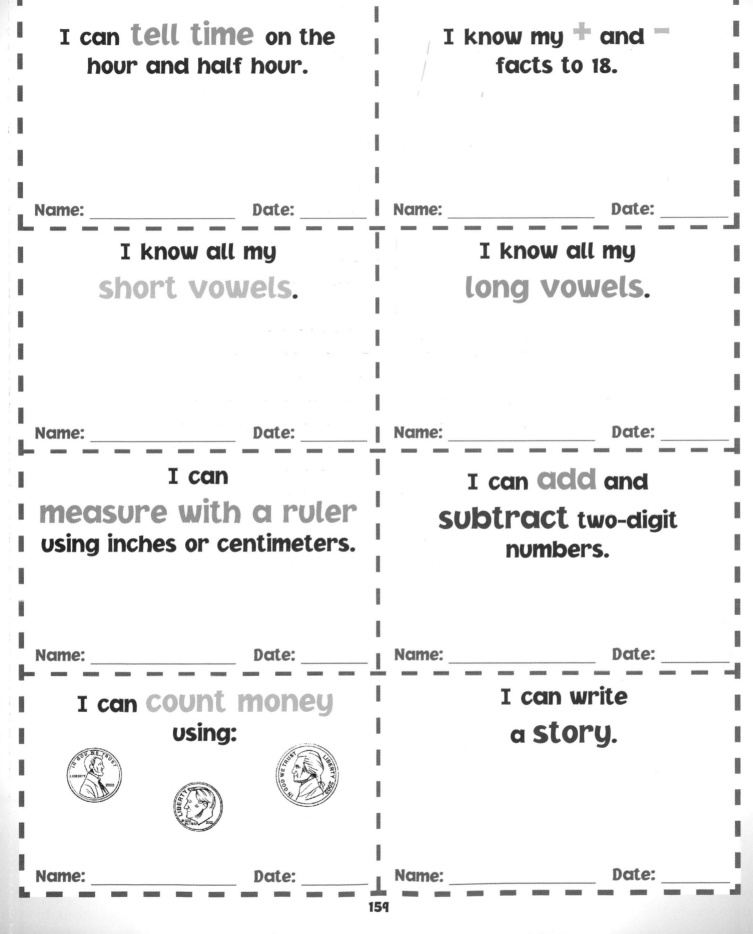

Name: ______________ Date: ________

I can write a story.

Name: ______________ Date: ________